a pinch of spice

A PINCH OF SPICE

Indian recipes from home

Happy Cooking!

Balwinder Kapila

Balwinder

Matador
9 Priory Business Park,
Wistow Road, Kibworth Beauchamp,
Leicestershire. LE8 0RX
Tel: 0116 279 2299
Email: books@troubador.co.uk
Web: www.troubador.co.uk/matador
Twitter: @matadorbooks

ISBN 978 1789017 373

British Library Cataloguing in Publication Data.
A catalogue record for this book is available from the British Library.

Typeset in Londrina and Lato.
Printed and bound in Malta by Gutenberg Press Ltd

Matador is an imprint of Troubador Publishing Ltd

CONTENTS

WHAT SHALL I COOK TODAY?

"What shall I cook today?" or, as my mum would say, 'ki khana pakona aj' - a question that I'm certain is asked by many people all over the world. Here are a few menu ideas for you – enjoy!

Brunch
omelette
spicy potatoes
mango chutney
toast
lassi

Lavish Sunday brunch
minced lamb
aubergines with potatoes
chickpeas
poori
yogurt
tomato and onion salad
lassi
fruit chaat

Sunday vegetarian brunch
potato-stuffed chapatis
yogurt
lemon and ginger pickle/mango pickle
(and a nice cup of tea)

Celebratory vegetarian dinner
potato, chickpea and yogurt salad
vegetable biryani
whole urid dhal
okra with onion and tomato
chapati/naan
raita
tomato and cucumber salad
coconut and coriander chutney
Indian ice cream

Weekend vegetarian dinner
chickpeas
stuffed aubergines
yogurt
chapati/rice
carrot and white radish salad
lemon and ginger pickle
vermicelli pudding

Weekday vegetarian dinner
yellow split mung beans
roasted cauliflower
rice or chapati
yogurt
fruit salad

Dinner party
Gujarati-style savoury cakes
chicken korma and/or red kidney beans
cauliflower with potatoes
tangy okra
plain rice
coconut and coriander chutney
carrot pudding

Dinner party
lamb curry
whole urid dhal
potatoes with spinach
plain rice/chapati
raita
tomato and onion salad
paneer balls in an aromatic syrup

Simple supper
red split lentils
courgettes with tomatoes and lemon
plain rice

Barbecue party
barbecued prawns
lamb kebabs
barbecued paneer
Gujarati-style potatoes
aubergines and red peppers with tamarind
naan
raita
tomato and cucumber salad
coconut and coriander chutney
mint chutney
fruit salad
pomegranate and yogurt dessert

Soirée/drinks evening
samosas/spicy potato fritters (pakoras)
cumin chicken
barbecued prawns
smoky aubergines on ciabatta
carrot and green chilli salad
tamarind chutney
coconut and coriander chutney
carrot and white radish salad

Girls' winter lunch
chana dhal with fresh crusty bread
rice pudding

Easy and impressive
fish in a fenugreek and yogurt coconut sauce
green beans
rice
coconut and coriander chutney
fruit salad

Tea for guests
samosas
spicy potato fritters (pakoras)
savoury crackers (mathis)
tamarind chutney
mango pickle
Indian fudge

Sunday lunch
lamb in a spicy sauce
stuffed peppers
yellow split chickpeas
chapati
yogurt
lemon and ginger pickle

Friday or Saturday night dinner
Biji's chicken
rice with peas
yogurt
tomato and onion salad
fruit salad

Store-cupboard staples
garam masala
chaat masala
lemon and ginger pickle
mango pickle

A day in advance
green beans with mustard seeds
Gujarati-style carrots and cabbage
roasted aubergines and red peppers
carrot and green chilli salad
mango chutney
tamarind chutney
Indian ice cream
pomegranate and yogurt dessert
Indian fudge

This book is dedicated to Aran and Amar, in memory of Aman.

INTRODUCTION

What's the first thing that springs to mind when you think of Indian cooking? The flavours? The colours? The wonderful spices and aromas, perhaps? Or do you think, "I love the food, but I couldn't cook an Indian meal, it's too hard"? Trust me: it isn't – and in this book, I'll prove it!

I learnt to cook from my mother when I was a child. She worked shifts, which meant that I would sometimes be responsible for preparing the family's evening meal. This would usually consist of chapati, vegetables, lentils, yogurt, salad and a pickle or chutney. Punjabi cuisine is mostly vegetarian. Occasionally we would have meat at home, usually chicken or lamb, and there was paneer (Indian cheese) for the non-meat eaters. A dessert very rarely featured unless it was a special occasion, in which case we would have kheer (rice pudding); otherwise we would finish off a meal with fresh fruit. In a Gurdwara (Sikh temple), meat is never served, in order to be as welcoming as possible to people of all cultures. Indeed, the tradition of seva, or service to your community, is what makes the sharing of food with others so very important in our lives.

Offering food to our guests is not only a duty; it's a pleasure. It was always open house when family, friends, and friends of friends, turned up unexpectedly – and still is. This custom of 'popping in' probably originates from the culture and sense of community life that my parents and others of their generation grew up with and valued so much. So if it was teatime, for example, pakoras (deep-fried fritters) were hastily made, as there was always flour in the larder and home-grown potatoes or spinach in the garden, with yogurt in the fridge. If there wasn't any tamarind to be found, ketchup would do. And if anyone arrived at breakfast time, particularly on a Sunday, there was never any doubt that my mother would be making alooa di parathe (potato-filled chapatis); just something simple, and yet really special, that my brothers and I could never have enough of. And when I became a mother, it was my turn to do the same for my own boys, who have always devoured them with the same enthusiasm, if not more.

My parents grew up on farms, and the tradition of growing their own vegetables continued when they came to this country. Whatever we didn't have space for in our back garden was bought from the local farm shop. Today, of course, most Indian vegetables and spices are readily available in Asian stores or any supermarket or farmers' market, but back in the 1950s and 60s, only a small number of Indian groceries sold more exotic vegetables in West London. Every other Friday evening, a delivery van with Indian groceries would park outside our house and we were able to top up our supplies – a convenience fifty years ahead of its time, although I took it for granted then.

Everything was homemade, using the freshest ingredients. Whenever my parents travelled home to the Punjab, they brought tastes of India back with them: large tins of achaar (pickle), made with lemons or mangoes, specially prepared by an aunt, a bag of gur (unrefined sugar), juicy gana (sugar cane) and fresh amb (mangoes). Masalas and spices were all ground at home; buying them already prepared was unheard of. Big bags of spices were emptied and spread out on trays in the summer, left to dry in the sun, and then ground in the most enormous pestle and mortar, carried all the way from India.

Although I grew up on traditional Punjabi cuisine, many of our ingredients such as ginger, garlic, cumin, turmeric and black pepper are found in most parts of India. Regional cuisine varies, depending not only on climate and landscape, but also on the religious and cultural differences brought about by India's many rulers, such as the Mughals, the Portuguese and the British. For instance, wheat is popular in the Punjab, rice in southern India, coconut and fish in Kerala, chilli in Rajasthan, pulses and pickles in Gujarat, and so on.

Spices were also used medicinally. My family frequently used fresh ginger and garlic to keep us healthy: cloves to numb toothache, fennel seeds to aid digestion and carom seeds for an upset tummy. Turmeric was applied to wounds and swellings – I used to wonder why I was the only child going to school with yellow knees!

Leaving home at eighteen, living on a student budget and sharing a small kitchen with limited facilities, I had to adapt my cooking and become more creative. That was when I started using a one-pot cooking method for beans and lentils, to save time. I enjoyed them as a hearty soup with Western-style bread, rather than chapati, as an accompaniment. Dishes that would have been barbecued were grilled instead and accompanied by a simple salad and potatoes. I also discovered that you could spice up shop-bought yogurt to make a decent raita. Living in halls of residence in the early 80s, this was as close to the comfort of home as I could get.

For years, my friends have been asking for the secret to Indian food, but, as a British person who grew up in an Indian family, I didn't think there was any particular secret; it all seemed perfectly natural. The trouble sometimes seemed to be that people were using the right ingredients in the wrong way. When I was asked if I would give cooking lessons to show how it was done, I tried to explain that it was easy. I think perhaps the idea of using unfamiliar spices and ingredients, coupled with visions of standing by the stove for hours on end, made it all seem too much of a challenge for many people. I hope this book helps dispel some of the myths, and inspires you to be adventurous and enthusiastic about trying these recipes.

When I decided to write a cookery book in memory of our son Aman, many friends were keen to help. A few hastily scribbled recipes eventually began to transform themselves into a book. Cooking together, testing recipes in each other's homes, sharing ideas of food and culture, photography masterclasses and proofreading all played their part. There has been a lot of laughter, and a few tears too, of course. Aman has always been very much a part of our journey.

In fact, creating this book has actually developed my understanding of Indian food. For me, it really is all about the spices. Balancing rich, spicy flavours with a cooler, more refreshing taste, and knowing how to make a dish that is not too salty, too chilli or too bland, are skills learnt over many years by the best Indian cooks. I have recently become vegetarian and people often wonder how I am able to create the meat dishes with confidence. I always reply that I watched my mother and aunts cooking as I was growing up. The spices – all the ingredients, in fact – were added instinctively; everything was measured simply by recognising flavours and aromas. Unfamiliar dishes were prepared by trial and error; recipe books just didn't exist in Indian homes. Writing this book brought me into contact with cooking techniques and recipes that have been with me since childhood but that I had not fully understood. They are now firmly established in my kitchen, motivating me to learn more about my culinary heritage. All this has made me realise how simple things can be: the more I cooked and checked the recipes, the more I wondered why I'd ever worried about it all.

It has also been a lot of fun investigating how much I should add of a particular ingredient – and interpreting the responses from my mother and aunts: torak (a little), bhot ni or jada ni (not too much), kafi (quite a lot), or thorak jada (a little bit more)! On one such occasion, and being aware of the 'love it or hate it' association Indian sweetmeats carry, I had three different versions of besan (Indian-style fudge) cooking simultaneously. These were then scored by an Indian friend, an English friend and a French friend. After considerable discussion of East meets West, I have chosen the recipe that appeals most to all palates. Serving it later for tea to my parents, aunt and uncle, I was relieved to have the final seal of approval.

Most of the dishes in this book are from the Punjab region of northern India. I have combined traditional Indian home-cooked food with other recipes that I have developed over the years. I hope you will enjoy serving your family and friends the dishes that I have so much enjoyed serving to mine.

Balwinder Kapila

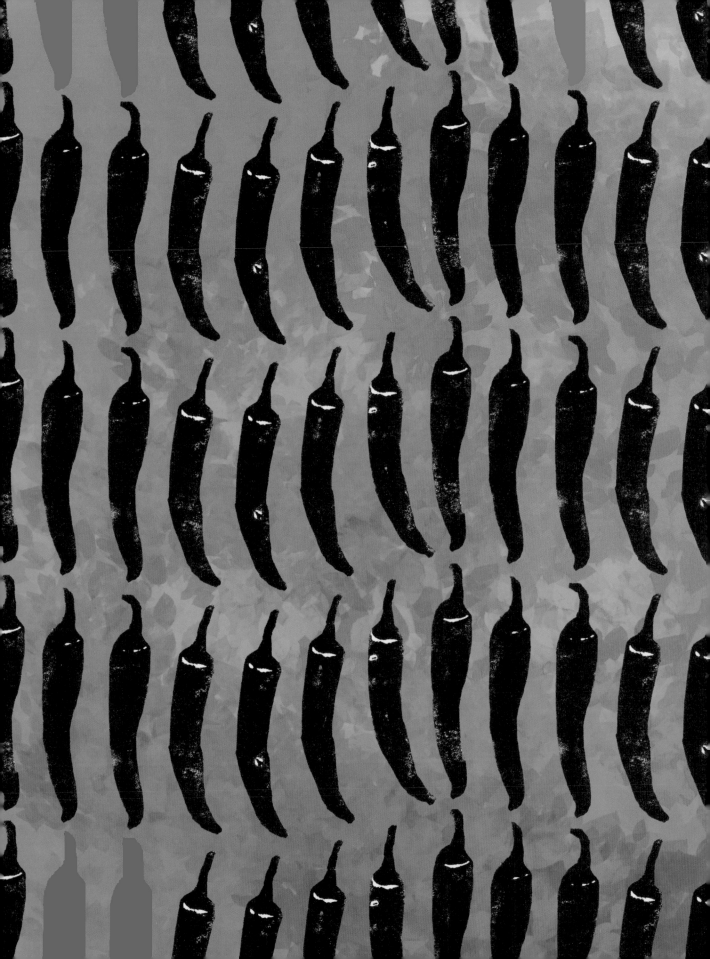

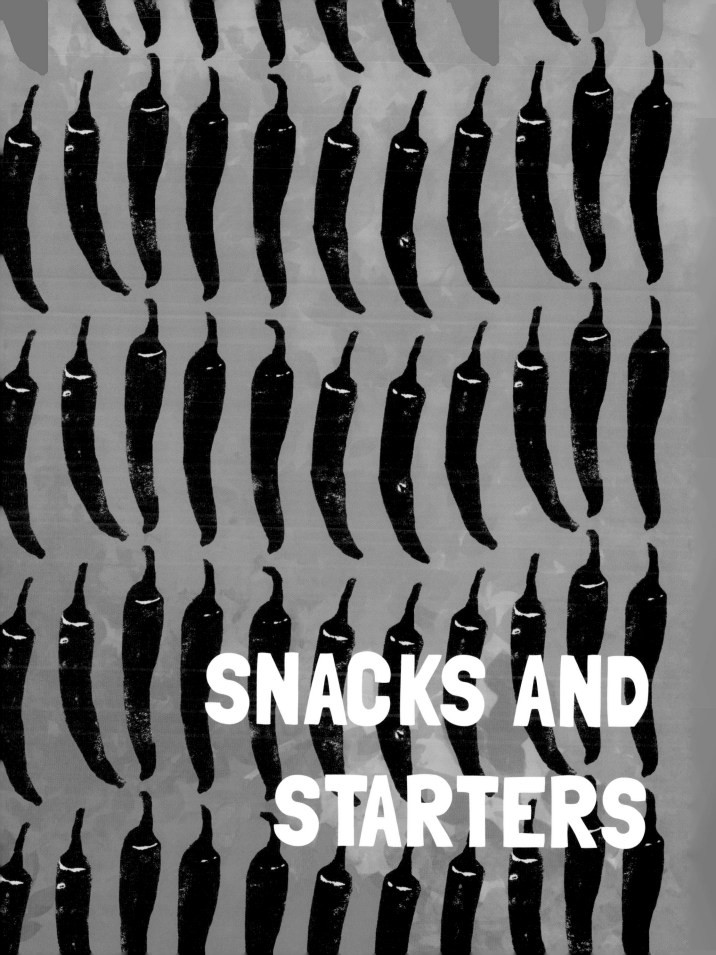

SNACKS AND STARTERS

Fried, grilled or baked – small dishes for every occasion

I've grouped these together as they are so versatile. Depending on the time of day, or the occasion, they can be served either as snacks or starters. For me as a youngster, when we had friends and family over for dinner, it really meant having tea first, in the late afternoon, before   moving onto the 'real' meal. So, out would come our special cups and saucers, reserved for these gatherings. The plates, similarly held back for such occasions, were laden with lovingly prepared pakoras, samosas and mathis and served with a selection of chutneys. These treats were relished by our visitors – offering yet another reason to love days like those. As if this wasn't enough for your taste buds, you could round this off with a cup of Indian chai (tea). Sipping the steaming, aromatic tea, on top of a tongue tingling from the food is one of my favourite 'pain as pleasure' moments! And when you felt that you should keep some space in your tummy for the dinner that was yet to come, your hosts would more often than not convince you to have "just one more".

Whenever these savouries were prepared for big parties, friends and relatives would bend to the task of chopping, rolling, filling and frying. I remember these as fun occasions with lots of laughter, where news about families was shared, with recipes compared and sometimes improved upon. How else could you prepare a hundred or more of these delicious snacks?

Aloo papri chaat, sholay tikki and chilli paneer can be enjoyed as starters but would make great light meals too. What these dishes all share is their sweet and spicy flavour, though their textures vary – light, flaky, crunchy, soft and crispy.

Jeera chicken, barbecue prawns and sheekh kebabs are lavish-tasting finger foods but are still simple to prepare. They will also work well for a drinks evening, served with some of the other snacks and lots of different chutneys. For the strong – or the foolish! – serve some green chillies on the side.

So, let's begin...

JEERA CHICKEN
Cumin chicken

This dish is all about getting the texture of the chicken spot on – it should be moist enough not to burn in the pan but dry enough not to become runny. The perfect finished dish will be slightly browned with a thick crust of spices. It's a versatile recipe as it can be eaten with other Indian dishes, cold in a salad, in a sandwich or even as a filling for pitta bread. This would be great at a party or a buffet, where you could serve it as finger food. Using a heat diffuser (page 267) helps to cook the chicken slowly and evenly.

Serves 8-10

3 tbsp oil
30g ginger, finely chopped
3 cloves garlic, finely chopped
3 green chillies, finely chopped

1 tbsp ground cumin
1 tsp ground black pepper
½ tsp salt
24 chicken wings

Heat the oil in a large karahi or saucepan on a low heat. Add the ginger, garlic and chillies and fry gently for 2 minutes. Add the cumin, black pepper and salt and continue frying for a further 2 minutes. It will look quite dry at this stage. Add a splash of water if it is sticking to the pan.

Add the chicken wings and brown on a moderately high heat for about 4-5 minutes. This is where to place the heat diffuser on the stovetop, if you're using one. Lower the heat and cover for an hour to an hour and a half, or until the chicken is cooked through and just starting to fall off the bone. Stir occasionally.

VEGETABLE SAMOSAS

This is a light and flaky oven-baked alternative to the traditionally deep-fried Punjabi samosa. The crispy filo pastry is a perfect foil for the surprise of flavours wrapped inside. The soft, spiced potato, with subtle hints of lemon, will make you want to eat more and more. And if that isn't enough for your palate, add a great big dollop of tamarind chutney (page 214) and let the flavours unfold.

There are different ways to eat a samosa. You can eat them with a knife and fork or, as I prefer, you can use your hands and nibble away in your own time. If you want, you can pop the whole thing in your mouth in one go, but be careful if they are straight out of the oven and piping hot.

Remember that filo pastry dries out very easily, so keep it wrapped up until you are ready to use another sheet. The samosas can be prepared in advance and cooked just before serving. *Photo page 22.*

Makes about 24

700g all-purpose potatoes,
   boiled and mashed
1 tsp salt
juice of 1 lemon
3 tbsp oil
1 tbsp cumin seeds
1 small onion, chopped
50g ginger, very finely chopped
4 green chillies, finely chopped

1 tsp ground black pepper
1½ tsp garam masala
250g frozen peas
a handful of coriander leaves,
   roughly chopped
a little oil, to grease the baking
   trays and for the pastry
250g filo pastry, cut into
   10cm x 25cm rectangles

Mix together the mashed potato, salt and lemon juice in a large bowl and set aside.

Heat the oil in a karahi or saucepan on a medium heat and add the cumin seeds, allowing them to sizzle for a few seconds. Add the onions and fry for 2 minutes. Lower the heat slightly and then add the ginger and chillies. Stir for a minute before adding the black pepper and garam masala. Add the peas and continue stirring for another couple of minutes. Add the mashed potato mixture and cook for a further few minutes, checking that all the ingredients are mixed thoroughly. Transfer to a bowl and allow to cool to room temperature. Gently stir in the chopped coriander.

Preheat the oven to 180°C/350°F/Gas Mark 4.

Lightly oil two baking trays. Lay a sheet of the filo pastry on a board and brush a little oil along the edges of the pastry. Put a tablespoon of the potato mixture towards one end of the sheet and then carefully take one corner of the pastry and fold it over the filling diagonally, so that you have a triangular shape. Then fold it back over on itself. Seal the edges together by folding the bottom layer of pastry over the top. Lightly brush the top face of each samosa with oil.

Place the samosas on the trays and bake in the oven for 15-18 minutes until the edges of the pastry are crisp and golden.

PAKORAS
Potato fritters

These crunchy battered fritters are completely moreish. You can make them with other vegetables such as cauliflower, spinach or aubergine, but I adore the combination of the delicate potato flavour with the spicy batter. And let's face it, fried potatoes are always good.

Growing up, we didn't often have deep-fried snacks but I can remember great excitement on afternoons when my massis (mum's sisters) would come over for a massive cooking session with my mum. They would make pakoras, samosas (page 20) and pooris (page 190), which were treats reserved for special occasions. It was always a race with my brothers to be at the front of the queue when the pakoras were ready to come out of the pan. They were deliciously fresh, but we had to be careful our eyes weren't bigger than our tummies!

I add a little yogurt to my mixture to make the pakoras slightly softer, but if you want a crispier texture, omit the yogurt and add a little more water. Serve with tamarind chutney (page 214) or even tomato ketchup. *Photo page 26.*

You can make pakoras with the other vegetables as follows:

Spinach
Finely chop 200g spinach leaves. Add to the batter with the onions and potatoes.

Aubergine
Replace some or all of the potatoes with aubergines. Cut crossways into 5mm-thick circles and add to the batter with the onions.

Cauliflower
Replace some or all of the potatoes with small to medium-sized florets.

Serves 6-8
as a starter
or for chai-time

250g gram flour (besan), sieved
200ml water (or 250ml if omitting
   the yogurt)
100g natural yogurt
1 tbsp cumin seeds
1 tsp turmeric
2 tsp dried pomegranate seeds,
   (optional)
1 tbsp garam masala
1½ tsp salt

50g ginger, finely chopped
2 green chillies, finely chopped
a handful of coriander leaves,
   roughly chopped
1 small onion, thinly sliced
500g all-purpose potatoes, peeled
   and cut into 3mm-thick slices
   (about as thick as a £1 coin)
oil for deep-frying

Put the flour into a large bowl. Add the water and yogurt and whisk until you have a smooth batter. Add the cumin seeds, turmeric, pomegranate seeds, garam masala, salt, ginger, chillies and coriander. Mix well. Add the onions and potatoes and stir gently until the vegetables are coated with the batter.

Gradually heat the oil in a karahi or deep saucepan on a medium heat. Lower tablespoons of the mixture into the oil. It's important the pakoras don't stick to each other so, to avoid crowding them in, cook them in batches. Fry for 7-10 minutes until dark golden brown, turning over once or twice. Lift out with a slotted spoon and drain on kitchen paper. Serve piping hot.

MATHIS

Savoury crackers with crushed peppercorns and carom seeds

Mathis are distributed amongst family and friends to mark special occasions such as weddings and engagements. I recall making these for the first time when I was eight or nine years old. My mum and I were visiting my Aunty Sagoo, who was a very close family friend. She and my mother were like sisters and they would do everything together. They worked together, walked to town together, cooked special foods together and often they would choose the same fabric to be made into a salwaar kameez (Indian trousers and tunic) and then wear them at the same time! My aunt's sister-in-law had also joined us. We were there to prepare a huge batch of mathis which were then going to be divided between our families. I was excited because I was going to help the adults and felt very grown up. Added to that, I could boast to my brothers that "I made these" – well, at least I rolled one or two out!

Try these with a hot cup of tea and you'll find that the flavours of the spices are so intensified, you'll be smacking your lips. Also delicious with mango pickle (page 226).

Makes about 16	150g plain flour, sieved, plus a little extra for dusting	1 tsp carom seeds
	½ tsp salt	30ml oil
	1½ tsp black peppercorns, crushed	50-60ml water
		oil, for deep-frying

Mix the flour, salt, peppercorns and carom seeds in a large bowl. Add the oil and water. Knead until you have a stiff dough. The dough will be crumbly and messy to start with, but eventually it will hold together so don't be tempted to add more water too soon.

Divide the dough into 4 equal parts. Very lightly sprinkle a little flour onto the work surface and roll out each portion to the thickness of a £1 coin. Using a pastry cutter, cut into circles about 6cm in diameter. Lightly prick each circle twice with a fork to prevent them from puffing up when frying.

Gradually heat the oil in a karahi or deep saucepan on a medium heat. In small batches, fry the circles for approximately 2-3 minutes, or until a light golden colour, turning over once. Lift out carefully with a slotted spoon and drain on kitchen paper. The mathis will crisp up as they cool and will keep for up to two weeks in an airtight container.

[L to R] Aunty Sagoo, Nanny and Biji, at home in Hounslow, Middlesex (1984)

BARBECUED PRAWNS

These prawns are a guaranteed favourite for summer barbecues (although, at a pinch, they can be cooked in a frying pan or griddle). This particular blend of ingredients creates a spicy and smoky dish, just a little charred on the outside and nice and juicy on the inside. The marinade should be applied just before cooking so that the prawns retain their firmness and bite. If you have the time and inclination, deveining and butterflying them (page 264) will help the marinade really cover the prawns all over.

Serve hot off the barbecue with coconut and coriander chutney (page 204).

Serves 6

150g natural yogurt
15g ginger, finely chopped
2 cloves garlic, finely chopped
¼ tsp chilli flakes

1 tsp ground cumin
500g peeled raw king prawns
1 tsp salt

Put the yogurt into a large bowl and stir in the ginger, garlic, chilli flakes and ground cumin. Add the prawns and carefully coat them with the yogurt marinade. Thread the prawns onto the skewers.

Preheat the barbecue to a medium heat. Barbecue the prawns for 4-5 minutes, flipping them halfway through. You will know they are cooked when they turn pink all over.

SHEEKH KEBABS
Lamb kebabs

These fiery kebabs are the perfect barbecue food for a warm summer's evening. Serve with raita (page 224) if you think you might need cooling down, although mint chutney (page 216) will give them even more of a zing! Start your preparations well ahead, ideally the night before, to give the flavours a chance to develop. The lamb can then either be shaped to size or wrapped around metal skewers (or sheekhs as they are known in India).

Can also be served as a main course.

Serves 6

400g lamb shoulder, minced
1 small onion, finely chopped
30g ginger, finely chopped
2 green chillies, finely chopped
a handful of coriander leaves, chopped
½ tsp ground black pepper

1 tsp garam masala
½ tsp salt
2 slices bread, soaked in water for 5 minutes, drained and squeezed of excess water
a little oil (if using metal skewers)

Line a sieve or colander with muslin or a thin cotton tea towel and place over a large bowl. Put the onions, ginger and coriander onto the cloth and, using a spoon, press down to push the juice through into the bowl. Discard the juice. Mix all the ingredients (apart from the oil) together in a large bowl. Knead gently for a minute or so. Be careful not to overwork the mixture as you don't want it to end up as a heavy mass. Wet the palms of your hands and press the meat into shape – a little thinner than a jumbo sausage and about 12cm long. Alternatively, if using skewers, brush them lightly with the oil and, again with wet hands, press the meat onto them.

Cover and chill the kebabs in the fridge for at least an hour. Take the kebabs out of the fridge about 15 minutes before barbecuing so as to ensure the meat is at room temperature (to allow for even cooking).

Preheat the barbecue to a medium heat. Grill for about 7-10 minutes, turning frequently. The outside should be lightly charred and the inside soft and cooked. Carefully slide them off the skewers to serve.

ALOO PAPRI CHAAT

Potato, chickpea and yogurt salad on a crispy base (Gurdwara Ladies' recipe)

Indian street food offers many heavenly possibilities and aloo papri chaat is one of the most popular. In any Indian city you will find street vendors manning carts from which they will prepare your food to order. Go to someone selling this dish and in a matter of seconds you'll have a lip-smacking snack of tender potatoes and chickpeas, crunchy papri, cool yogurt and sweet, tart tamarind. You can even choose how sweet, salty, sour or chilli you want this dish. Aloo papri chaat is actually a combination of three recipes: papri (described below), chaat masala (page 254) and tamarind chutney (page 214). To make things easier, you can buy the papri from most Indian food stores, so there really is no excuse to miss out. This makes a great appetiser for a big crowd as all the different parts can be prepared in advance and assembled just before serving.

This recipe was given to me by the lovely ladies I used to teach at the Gurdwara in Reading, who always spoilt me with all the delicious food they prepared there. *Photo page 38.*

Serves 6

For the papri
1 box of shop-bought papri
or
200g plain flour, sieved, plus a
    little extra for dusting
2 tsp oil
¼ tsp salt
130ml water
oil, for deep-frying

For the chaat
1 x 400g tin of chickpeas, drained,
    rinsed and pat-dried with kitchen
    paper (240g drained weight)
250g all-purpose potatoes,
    peeled and boiled until just
    tender, cooled and cut into
    1cm cubes
½ small onion, quite finely
    chopped
750g natural yogurt
1 tbsp *chaat masala* (page 254)
tamarind chutney (page 214)
a handful of coriander leaves,
    chopped, to garnish

Prepare the papri
Put the flour in a large mixing bowl. Add the oil, salt and water. Knead for about 5 minutes until you have a firm but pliable dough. Shape into a ball and then cover the bowl with a damp cloth (or cling film). Leave to rest for about 15 minutes.

Knead again gently for a minute. Divide the dough into 4 equal portions to make it easier to work with. Sprinkle a little flour onto the work surface and roll out each portion to the thickness of a 20p coin. Using a pastry cutter, cut into circles about 3cm in diameter. Lightly prick each circle twice with a fork to prevent them from puffing up when frying.

Gradually heat the oil for deep-frying in a karahi or deep saucepan on a medium heat. In small batches, gently slide the circles of dough into the oil and fry for 1-2 minutes or until crisp and golden brown. Lift out carefully with a slotted spoon and drain on kitchen paper. Allow the papri to cool completely.

Assemble the dish
Cover the base of a shallow serving dish with the papri. Spoon the chickpeas evenly over the papri, followed by the potatoes and onions. Cover completely with the yogurt. Sprinkle the chaat masala over the yogurt and then drizzle over the tamarind chutney as evenly as possible. Garnish with the coriander and serve.

CHILLI PANEER

Unlike all the other recipes in this book, this vegetarian dish is an intriguing blend of cooking techniques and ingredients originating from the small Chinese community that has been living in Kolkata for over a century. Other well-known Indo-Chinese dishes include chow mein noodles, fried rice and Manchurian chicken (all done with an Indian twist).

Chilli paneer is spicy, salty and sweet through the generous use of chillies, soy sauce and tomato ketchup. The sugars from the ketchup caramelise and form a delicious smoky crust on the paneer and peppers. Frying the paneer before adding it to the other vegetables helps it to retain a bite. *Photo page 42.*

Serves 6-8

For the paneer
approximately 500g *paneer cubes*
  (pages 257-8)
or
500g shop-bought paneer,
  cut into 2cm cubes

For the vegetables
75ml oil
40g ginger, very finely chopped
4 large cloves garlic,
  finely chopped
4 thin green chillies, thinly sliced
  on the diagonal

3 spring onions, thinly sliced on the
  diagonal, reserving the (very finely
  sliced) green part for garnishing
1 small red onion, quartered and
  thinly sliced
1 large red pepper, halved
  lengthways, seeds removed
  and diced into 2cm pieces
1 large green pepper, halved
  lengthways, seeds removed
  and diced into 2cm pieces
2 tbsp light soy sauce
2 tbsp ketchup

Heat the oil in a large karahi or frying pan on a medium heat. Fry the cubes of paneer in the oil, gently turning them so that all sides become lightly golden. Lift out with a slotted spoon and drain on kitchen paper.

Pour away most of the oil, keeping about 2 tbsp in the pan. Bring back to a medium heat and fry the ginger and garlic. Stir regularly and, when the mix is starting to colour, add the chillies, white spring onion slices and red onions. When the onions are translucent and just starting to colour, raise the heat to high. Add the peppers, stirring constantly for one minute. Add the soy sauce and ketchup and keep stirring for another minute until the ingredients are lightly caramelised. If the mixture starts to burn, add a very small amount of water.

Return the fried paneer to the pan, stir gently for three minutes and mix well. Transfer to a serving dish and garnish with the sliced green spring onions. Serve piping hot.

SHOLAY TIKKI
Chickpeas with potatoes

Sholay tikki and aloo papri chaat (page 36) have a lot in common. You will typically find both dishes on an Indian street food stall. They share many ingredients and flavours and they are similarly assembled. Back home in Britain, the piping hot tikkis and chickpeas, together with crisp tart onion, dollops of yogurt, and splashes of tamarind chutney make an impressive starter. Try replicating the street origins of this dish by presenting the components separately so your guests can help themselves and customise the flavours to their own individual taste.

You'll find your taste buds challenged in a wonderful way with contrasts of sweet and sour, hot and cold. Although I've described the traditional way to layer the various components of the dish, and this is the one I prefer, I've had a lot of fun over the years watching friends compare and debate on the right way to do it. My advice is – enjoy them any way you like!

If you're preparing the recipe using dried chickpeas, remember they will need soaking the night before.

Serves 8-10

For the tikkis
800g all-purpose potatoes,
  boiled and mashed
½ tsp salt
½ tsp ground black pepper
a little oil, to brush
  over the tikkis

To assemble the dish
chickpeas (page 104)
1 small onion,
  roughly chopped
500g natural yogurt
tamarind chutney (page 214)

Prepare the tikkis
Put the mashed potatoes in a large bowl and add the salt and black pepper. Form into 'cakes' about 1cm thick and about 5cm in diameter. Makes around 20 tikkis.

Brush both sides with the oil and place on a baking sheet. Grill under a gentle medium heat, turning once, until slightly crispy and lightly browned.

Assemble the dish
Place one or two tikkis on your plate. Then pile on a few tablespoons of the chickpeas, followed by a teaspoon of chopped onions, a dollop of yogurt and finally a sprinkle of tamarind chutney.

DHOKLA

Gujarati-style steamed savoury cakes

With this dish, 'the icing on the cake' is the tempered spices that are drizzled over at the end to bring out the flavour of these light and airy steamed vegetarian snacks.

If you don't have a steamer, use a wide, deep pan and place an upturned heatproof bowl or wok stand in the bottom. Check that the tin you are using to cook the batter fits into the pan. I use either a 2lb loaf tin or a 20cm round cake tin, both work equally well. The mixture will rise a little so once the batter is in, you'll need to leave a space of at least 1cm on top.

Enjoy with coconut and coriander chutney (page 204) or tamarind chutney (page 214) – or both! *Photo page 48.*

Serves 8

For the cake
150g gram flour (besan), sieved
75g semolina
200ml water
90g natural yogurt
½ tsp turmeric
1 tbsp caster sugar
¾ tsp salt
1 tsp carom seeds
20g ginger, finely chopped
2 green chillies, finely chopped
1 tbsp oil, plus a little extra
  to grease the cake tin
juice of ½ lemon
½ tsp bicarbonate of soda
½ tsp chilli powder

For the garnish
2 tbsp oil
1 tbsp mustard seeds
15 curry (neem) leaves,
  fresh or dried
3 green chillies,
  sliced on the diagonal
2 tbsp water
a handful of coriander leaves,
  chopped, to garnish

Prepare the cake
Put the flour and semolina into a large bowl. Add the water and yogurt. Whisk until you have a smooth batter, similar to the consistency of a cake mixture.

Add the turmeric, sugar, salt, carom seeds, ginger and chillies. Mix well. Stir in the oil, lemon juice and bicarbonate of soda. The batter will fizz slightly.

Lightly grease the tin. Pour in the batter, sprinkle over the chilli powder and place the tin on the upturned bowl (or stand) in a deep saucepan. Now fill the pan with hot water until it reaches just below the base of the tin. The water should be bubbling away gently. Cover and steam for 12-15 minutes. Check that it is cooked through by using a knife or cocktail stick. If it comes out clean, your dish is done. Remove from the steamer and set aside.

Prepare the garnish
Heat the oil in a small pan on a medium heat. Add the mustard seeds. When they crackle, add the neem leaves and sliced chillies. Fry for 10-15 seconds. Pour in the hot water and turn off the heat.

Put the dish together
Remove the cake tin and place the dhokla on a plate. Pour over the garnish of tempered spices and leave for about half an hour to allow the cake to become really moist and flavoursome. Sprinkle over the chopped coriander. Cut into squares or diamond shapes and serve still warm or, if you prefer, allow it to cool completely.

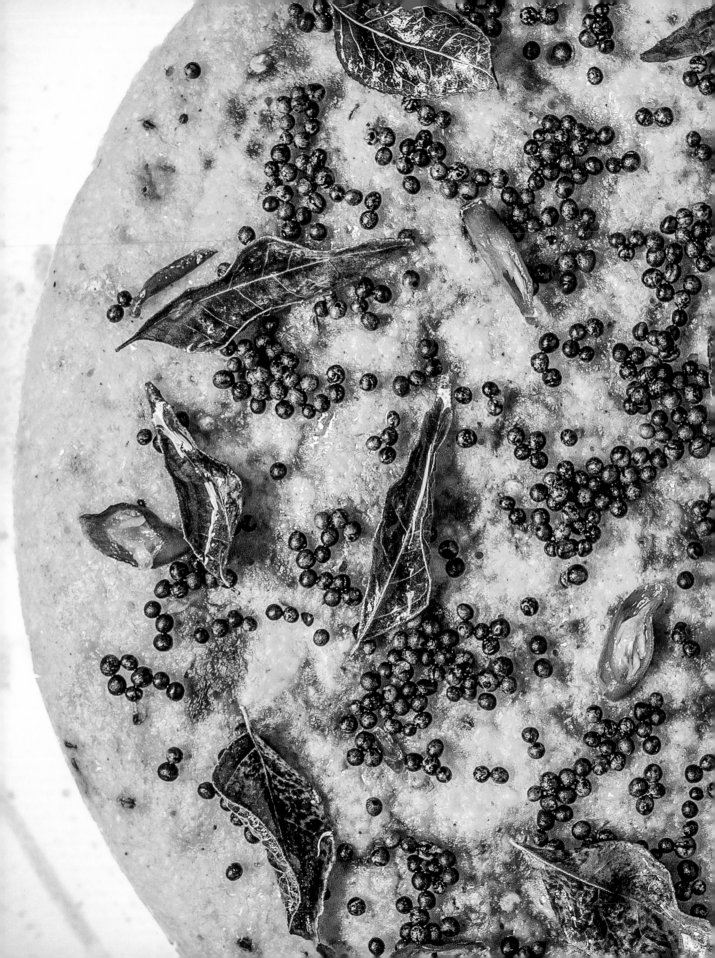

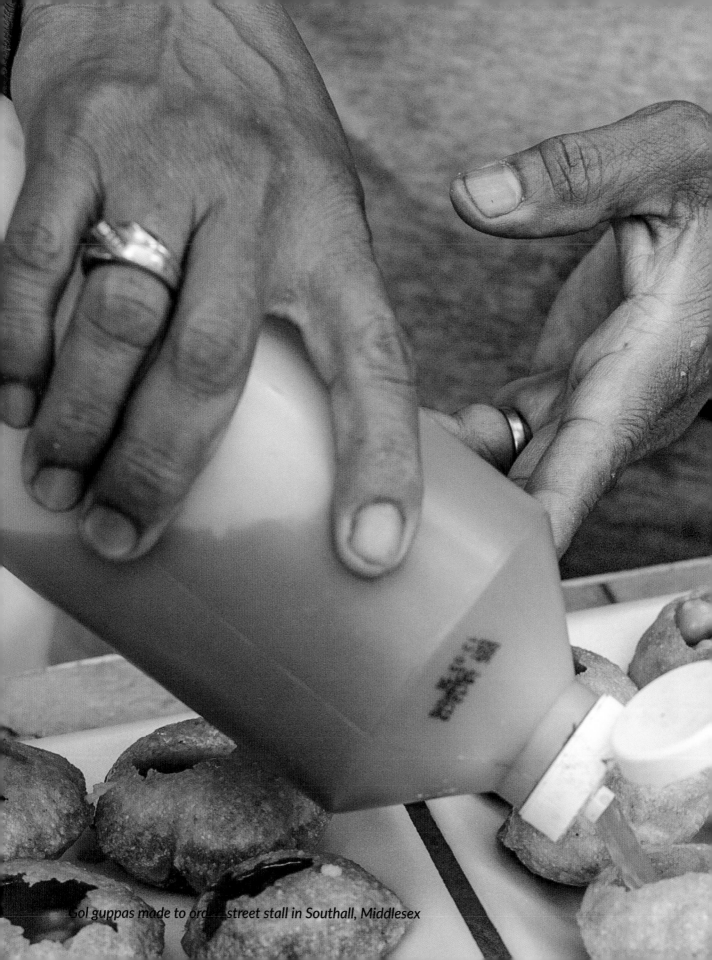

Gol guppas made to order, street stall in Southall, Middlesex

MEAT AND FISH

From simple, everyday recipes, to the gourmet dishes of Indian royalty

Meat and fish have always been special foods because, traditionally, poor people couldn't always afford them. This list of dishes is at the heart of Indian cuisine. Although many spices are commonly used all over India, the cooking techniques, flavours and textures of the recipes can vary immensely from region to region.

In northern parts of the country (including the Punjab, New Delhi and Uttar Pradesh), meat and fish were prepared with an exotic blend of spices, inherited from the Mughlai style of cooking, originating from Central Asia. The meat was often marinated in yogurt and cooked in clay ovens known as tandoors. Ground or minced meat was used to make kebabs, which were cooked over the open fire. Biryanis and pilaus reflected the splendour of this era where any number of spices, herbs, fruit and nuts were combined with meat and rice to create elaborate dishes 'fit for a king'. Kormas were slow-cooked and richly flavoured with nuts and yogurt or cream.

In typical Punjabi dishes, a masala is created by gradually adding onions, ginger, garlic, fresh chillies, turmeric and, lastly, tomatoes. Some of the recipes call for a really thick sauce, so follow the instructions closely. Garam masala (page 256) is added either during the cooking process or sprinkled on top of the finished dish. In contrast, when staying further to the south in Kerala, I learnt that the sauces there are more often flavoured using coconut, tamarind, mustard seeds and neem leaves.

Although I've given recipes for certain meats and fish, many of them are interchangeable so go ahead and cook according to your own preferences.

BIJI'S CHICKEN

Oh, so Punjabi... My mum, or Biji as we call her, would make this dish on a Friday night and any leftovers would be enjoyed by whoever got to it first the following morning.

Cooked gently, the chicken is able to absorb all the rich flavours of the sauce. Chapati (page 182) is the everyday accompaniment to this dish but, to make it really special, try rice with peas (page 198).

Serves 6

5 tbsp oil
1 tbsp cumin seeds
3 medium onions, finely chopped
60g ginger, finely chopped
6 cloves garlic, finely chopped
2 green chillies, finely chopped
500ml freshly boiled water
1 tsp turmeric

1 tsp salt
550g ripe tomatoes, blended
   or 400g passata
1.5kg skinless chicken thighs
   or 1 x 2kg whole chicken,
   skinned and jointed
1 tbsp garam masala

Heat the oil in a large karahi or wide saucepan on a medium heat and add the cumin seeds, allowing them to sizzle for a few seconds. Add the onions and fry for 5 minutes. Lower the heat slightly and fry for a further 8-10 minutes. The onions should be dark golden.

Add the ginger, garlic and chillies and stir thoroughly for 2 minutes. Add 100ml of the water and stir for a few minutes before adding the turmeric and salt. Add another 100ml of water. Continue stirring for a further 5 minutes. Add the tomatoes and cook on a medium-low heat for 15-20 minutes, stirring from time to time. You'll know it's ready when the sauce is thick enough to slide slowly off the sides of the pan. If the sauce does begin to stick to the pan, lower the heat and add a splash of water.

Add the chicken pieces and brown them all over on a medium heat, making sure that they are coated with the sauce. This will take about 10 minutes. Add the remaining 300ml of water. Cover with a lid, leaving a slight gap, and cook on a low heat for 15 minutes, stirring occasionally. Replace the lid to cover the pan completely and simmer for a further 20-25 minutes, stirring once or twice, until the chicken is cooked through. Sprinkle the garam masala over at the end of the cooking time and give it one more gentle stir.

My mum, Biji (1957)

[L to R] Ram, Sukh, me (age 4) and Major (1963)

CHICKEN BIRYANI

Virtually all of the south and south-eastern Asian countries have their own versions of biryani. What is common to them all is the technique of combining meat, fish, vegetables, or even paneer, cooked in spices among layers of fluffy rice. Your guests will be tempted by the fragrance of the biryani wafting through the air long before it is presented to them. The white grains of rice, offset by splashes of saffron-yellow, crown the richly flavoured chicken. Crispy onions provide a satisfying contrast to the texture of the other ingredients.

This recipe might look complicated but it is well worth the effort. After all, it was a dish created for the Mughal emperors, the royalty of historic India. To impress, serve the biryani on a big platter with accompanying dishes of raita (page 226), tomato and cucumber salad (page 206) and coconut and coriander chutney (page 204). There is also a splendid vegetarian version of this recipe on page 130.

If cooking on the stovetop, place the pan on a heat diffuser (see page 267) or on a cast-iron frying pan so that the meat and rice cook slowly and evenly. Don't be put off by the long list of ingredients. To make it easier for yourself, measure out the spices beforehand. *Photo page 62.*

Serves 6-8

For the chicken
4 tbsp oil
1.5kg skinless chicken thighs
100g ginger, finely chopped
6 cloves garlic, finely chopped
2 green chillies, finely chopped
1 tsp green cardamom pods, husks
    removed and seeds finely ground
1 tsp black peppercorns
8 cloves
3 black cardamom pods
1 cinnamon stick, about 5cm
3 bay leaves
2 tbsp ground cumin
2 tbsp ground coriander
1 tbsp turmeric
1 tsp salt
500g natural yogurt

For the onions
150ml oil
3 medium onions, finely sliced

For the rice
350g basmati rice, rinsed and
    soaked in cold water for
    30 minutes
1 tbsp cumin seeds
4 black cardamom pods
4 green cardamom pods
1 cinnamon stick, about 5cm
1 bay leaf
1 tsp salt
at least 2 litres cold water

To assemble the dish
a knob of butter, to grease the pan
a generous pinch of saffron
    strands, soaked in 4 tbsp
    hot milk
a handful of mint leaves,
    roughly chopped
a handful of coriander leaves,
    roughly chopped
5 x 1 tsp unsalted butter

Prepare the chicken layer
Heat the oil in a large karahi or wide saucepan on a medium heat. Add the chicken, followed by all the spices in the order given above. Cook on medium heat until the chicken is lightly browned. This will take about 10-12 minutes. Stir in the yogurt, a tablespoon at a time, and cook for another couple of minutes. Cover with a lid, leaving a slight gap, and simmer on a low heat for 20-25 minutes or until the chicken is cooked through, stirring occasionally. The sauce should be just thick enough to coat the chicken. Set aside.

Prepare the onion
Heat the oil in a large karahi or deep-sided frying pan on a medium heat. Add the onions and fry for about 10-15 minutes, stirring so that they do not stick to the pan. When done, they should be soft in the middle and dark golden brown on the outside (but not burnt).

Remove from the heat with a slotted spoon and spread out on kitchen paper. Take some more kitchen paper and press down on the onions to remove any excess oil. As they cool, they will become crispy. Set aside.

Prepare the rice
Drain the rice and put in a large pan with the spices. Add the water and bring to the boil, then simmer for 4-5 minutes. The rice should be only partially done, soft on the outside and firm in the middle, as it will cook fully later. Remove from the heat and drain the excess water.

Assemble the biryani
If baking, preheat the oven to 180°C/350°F/Gas Mark 4.

Generously butter a large heavy-bottomed saucepan or ovenproof dish with a tight-fitting lid. Arrange the chicken evenly on the bottom and scatter half the fried onions on top. Sprinkle over the chopped mint and coriander leaves followed by half of the rice. Drizzle half of the saffron milk over, followed by a layer of the remaining rice and a final sprinkle of the saffron milk. Finish by dotting the small knobs of butter on top.

Cover the dish with baking parchment (or foil) before placing the lid on, as you want to retain as much steam as possible to ensure it all cooks properly. If cooking on the hob, place the pan on a heat diffuser on a very low heat for 30-35 minutes, by which time your rice and chicken should be done. Alternatively, place in the oven and cook for 35-45 minutes.

Leave to stand for 10 minutes before removing the lid. Spoon onto a serving platter and garnish with the remaining crispy onions.

BARBECUED CHICKEN

If you barbecue chicken regularly, this will make a fantastic alternative to your normal recipe, and it's a breeze to prepare. The yogurt in the marinade tenderises the meat and keeps it moist, as well as forming a crispy seal when grilled. It's best to marinate the chicken a day in advance so that the flavours really penetrate. Serve the pieces whole, or slice them up and add to a tomato salad with a sprinkling of fragrant coriander and mint leaves.

Serves 6-8

120g natural yogurt
50g ginger, finely chopped
4 cloves garlic, finely chopped
½ tsp chilli flakes
1 tsp ground black pepper

2 tbsp ground cumin
1 tbsp paprika
1½ tsp salt
1.5kg skinless chicken thighs
   or 1.2kg skinless thigh fillets

If using whole thighs, slash the chicken so that the marinade gets into the meat.

Put the yogurt into a large bowl and stir in the ginger, garlic, chilli flakes, black pepper, cumin, paprika and salt. Add the chicken and coat it with the yogurt marinade. Cover and place in the fridge for at least 3 hours (ideally overnight). Take the chicken out of the fridge about 20-30 minutes before barbecuing to ensure the meat is at room temperature (to allow for even cooking).

Preheat the barbecue to a medium heat. Grill for 2 minutes on each side, then cook for a further 12-15 minutes (longer if using whole thighs), turning once or twice. Check that the chicken is ready by using a skewer to pierce the thickest part of the meat to see that the juices run clear.

CHICKEN KORMA

This beautifully spiced dish is another that has its origins in the Mughal dynasty, where it was sometimes even served with edible silver. Fragrant saffron and cardamom, combined with rich and lavish cream and almonds, make this something special to serve to your closest friends and family. And if you're vegetarian – like me – and simply cannot resist this sauce, omit the chicken and add a selection of cauliflower, butternut squash and red peppers.

Don't overdo the chilli: no spice should outshine the other.

Serves 6-8

4 tbsp oil
1 tbsp cumin seeds
1 cinnamon stick, about 5cm
2 star anise
2 bay leaves
1 tsp green cardamom pods, husks removed and seeds finely ground
1 medium onion, finely chopped
1 tbsp ground cumin
1 tsp turmeric
1 tsp ground black pepper
1 tbsp garam masala

1 tsp salt
a generous pinch of saffron strands, soaked in 200ml hot water
40g ginger, finely chopped
4 cloves garlic, finely chopped
2 green chillies, finely chopped
1.2kg skinless chicken thigh fillets, each fillet cut into three pieces
4 tbsp ground almonds
300ml single cream

Heat the oil in a large karahi or wide saucepan on a medium heat and add the cumin seeds, cinnamon stick, star anise, bay leaves and cardamom, allowing them to sizzle for a few seconds. Add the onions and fry for 4-5 minutes until just beginning to change colour.

Add the ground cumin, turmeric, pepper, garam masala and salt. Stir briskly for 2 minutes, adding 100ml of the saffron water when the ingredients start looking dry. Add the ginger, garlic and chillies and stir for a couple of minutes before adding the remaining 100ml of saffron water. Continue stirring for about 5 minutes until all the spices and flavours are absorbed into the onions.

Add the chicken and cook on a fairly high heat until browned. This will take about 5-7 minutes. If the chicken starts sticking to the pan, add a splash of water. Cover the pan and cook on a low heat for 15-20 minutes or until the chicken is done, adding the ground almonds halfway through.

In a separate pan, warm the cream gently then stir into the chicken and bring back to a simmer. Serve with plain rice (page 196) or naan (page 186) and roasted cauliflower (page 170) or one of the okra dishes (pages 152, 168).

CHICKEN PILAU

The beauty of this dish is that you are creating an irresistible feast in just one pot. It is prepared in a few simple steps so don't be deterred by the long list of ingredients. In all pilaus, the rice is fried with the rest of the ingredients. It absorbs these flavours and becomes incredibly fragrant. Serve with raita (page 224) and a vegetable of your choice. *Photo page 70.*

Serves 6-8

500g basmati rice, rinsed and soaked in cold water for 30 minutes
4 tbsp oil
1 tbsp cumin seeds
½ tsp black peppercorns
6 cloves
2 black cardamom pods
4 green cardamom pods, lightly crushed
1 cinnamon stick, about 5cm
2 star anise
2 bay leaves
3 medium onions, sliced

100g ginger, finely chopped
6 cloves garlic, finely chopped
4 green chillies, finely chopped
a generous pinch of saffron strands, soaked in 300ml hot water
1 tsp turmeric
1 tbsp garam masala
1½ tsp salt
1.5kg skinless chicken thighs
300g natural yogurt
750ml freshly boiled water, for cooking the rice

Heat the oil in a large karahi or heavy-based saucepan on a medium heat and add the cumin seeds, peppercorns, cloves, cardamom, cinnamon stick, star anise and bay leaves, allowing them to sizzle for a few seconds. Add the onions and fry for 4-5 minutes until just beginning to change colour.

Turn the heat down, add the ginger, garlic and chillies, and stir thoroughly for a few minutes. Add 100ml of the saffron water and stir for a few minutes before adding the turmeric, garam masala and salt. Stir briskly to prevent the spices from sticking to the bottom of the pan. Add another 100ml of the saffron water. Continue stirring for a further 5 minutes.

Add the chicken pieces and brown them all over on a medium heat making sure that they are coated with the sauce. This will take about 10 minutes. Add the remaining 100ml of saffron water and stir for a minute. Add the yogurt, a tablespoon at a time, and stir after each addition to prevent it from curdling. Cook gently for about 15 minutes on a medium heat, cover and continue cooking for another 15-20 minutes or until the chicken is tender.

Drain the rice and add to the chicken. Turn the heat to low and stir continuously for a few minutes until the rice just begins to take on a light golden hue. Add the 750ml of water to the pan and simmer until the bubbles of water have almost disappeared. Then cover and cook for approximately 10-15 minutes or until the water is completely absorbed and the rice is soft. It is important that the pan stays covered until the end of the cooking time so that the rice cooks evenly in the steam.

Allow to stand for 10 minutes before removing the lid.

KEEMA
Minced lamb with peas

This is one of those wonderful warm and filling dishes I loved in my childhood. Learning how quick and easy it was to make only made it all the more pleasurable. Use pieces of chapati to scoop up the keema or, for a more elaborate occasion, serve with pooris (page 190), with tomato and onion salad (page 212) on the side. Any leftover lamb is scrumptious on toast the next day.

Serves 6-8

2 tbsp oil
1 tbsp cumin seeds
1 black cardamom pod
1 cinnamon stick, about 5cm
30g ginger, finely chopped
4 cloves garlic, finely chopped
2 green chillies, finely chopped
1 tsp turmeric

1 tbsp garam masala
1 tsp salt
2 medium onions, chopped
1 tbsp tomato puree
250g ripe tomatoes, blended
  or 200g passata
800g lean minced lamb
300g fresh or frozen peas

Heat the oil in a medium-sized saucepan on a medium heat and then add the cumin seeds, cardamom and the cinnamon stick, allowing them to sizzle for a few seconds. Add the ginger, garlic, chillies, turmeric, garam masala and salt, and stir thoroughly. Add the onions and fry for 5-7 minutes until golden brown. Stir in the tomato puree and tomatoes and cook for another 5-7 minutes or until you have a thick sauce.

Add the lamb and cook until browned – this will take a few minutes. Use a wooden spoon to break up any lumps. Cover and cook on a low heat for a further 25-30 minutes, adding the peas halfway through the cooking time. Stir occasionally.

ROGAN GOSH
Lamb in a spicy sauce

If you want to serve up a wonderfully luxurious centrepiece that will go with a variety of accompaniments, then this is it: the definitive lamb curry. What makes this dish special lies in slow cooking and a thick, rich sauce.

Don't forget that the whole spices (cardamom, cinnamon and bay leaves) are there to add intensity to the recipe, not for eating. Although they have a wonderful aroma, they are very bitter when cooked and I have known my friends to spit them out after accidentally chewing them.

Serves 6

6 tbsp oil
1 tbsp cumin seeds
2 black cardamom pods
1 cinnamon stick, about 5cm
2 bay leaves
1 large onion, finely chopped
100g ginger, finely chopped
8 cloves garlic, finely chopped
4 green chillies, finely chopped

600ml freshly boiled water
1½ tsp turmeric
2 tbsp garam masala
1½ tsp salt
550g ripe tomatoes, blended
   or 400g passata
1kg boneless lamb shoulder,
   cut into 3cm chunks

Heat the oil in a large karahi or heavy-based saucepan on a medium heat and add the cumin seeds, cardamom, cinnamon stick and bay leaves, allowing them to sizzle for a few seconds. Add the onions and fry for 5 minutes. Lower the heat slightly and fry for a further 8 minutes. The onions should be dark golden.

Add the ginger, garlic and chillies and stir thoroughly. Add 100ml of the water and stir for a few minutes before adding the turmeric, garam masala and salt. Stir briskly. Add another 100ml of water. Continue stirring for a further 5 minutes.

Add the tomatoes and cook on a medium heat for 10-15 minutes, stirring from time to time. You'll know it's ready when the sauce is thick enough to slide slowly off the sides of the pan. If the sauce does begin to stick, lower the heat and add a splash of water.

Add the lamb and brown all over, stirring regularly for 5-7 minutes to ensure it is thoroughly coated with the sauce. Lower the heat, cover the pan completely and cook for an hour to an hour and a half or until the lamb is tender. During the cooking time, gradually add the remaining 400ml of water, stirring each time.

BARBECUED LAMB CHOPS

Lamb has always been the meat to mark a celebration in Indian culture and this recipe fits the bill perfectly – simple but full of flavour from a long marinating time. I have found lamb cutlets the easiest and tastiest to cook with: lovely tender meat with a neat little bone to hold onto, but chops taste just as good. Serve with mint chutney (page 216).

Serves 6-8

300g natural yogurt
50g ginger, finely chopped
4 cloves garlic, finely chopped
2 green chillies, finely chopped

2 tbsp garam masala
1½ tsp salt
1.5kg lamb cutlets or chops

Put the yogurt into a large bowl and stir in the ginger, garlic, chillies, garam masala and salt. Add the lamb and coat it with the yogurt marinade. Cover and place in the fridge for at least 3 hours (ideally overnight). Take the lamb out of the fridge about half an hour before barbecuing to ensure the meat is at room temperature (to allow for even cooking).

Preheat the barbecue to a medium heat. Lay the chops directly onto the grill. Barbecue for 2 minutes on each side and then for approximately 5 more minutes (for medium-done), turning once.

LAMB KOFTAS

Meatballs are popular in many cuisines. They are wholesome and comforting and can be made with cheaper cuts of meat. The North Indian version uses lamb but the recipe works equally well with chicken or pork. I like to brown the meatballs, as you get a fuller flavour and they're less likely to break up when added to the sauce, but, if you prefer a softer texture (and don't mind losing a couple), skip this step. As with any other meatball dish, it will be twice as enjoyable on a cold winter's day. Serve with rice (page 196) or chapati (182), yogurt (page 222) and cauliflower with potatoes (page 144). *Photo page 80.*

Serves 8-10

For the meatballs
1kg minced lamb
1 small onion, finely chopped
60g fresh ginger, finely chopped
2 cloves garlic, finely chopped
2 green chillies, finely chopped
1 tbsp cumin seeds
1 tbsp garam masala
1 tsp salt
a large handful of coriander leaves, finely chopped
2 slices bread, soaked in water for 5 minutes, drained and squeezed of excess water
4 tbsp oil, for browning the meatballs

For the sauce
4 tbsp oil
1 tbsp cumin seeds
4 medium onions, chopped
80g ginger, finely chopped
6 cloves garlic, finely chopped
4 green chillies, finely chopped
500ml freshly boiled water
1½ tsp turmeric
1 tbsp garam masala
1 tsp salt
800g ripe tomatoes, blended or 600g passata

Prepare the meatballs
Mix all the meatball ingredients together (apart from the oil) and knead for a minute or so. Wet the palms of your hands and form into balls about 5cm in diameter. Makes about 25 meatballs.

Brown the meatballs
Heat the oil in a large frying pan and brown the meatballs over a medium heat for about 5 minutes. Depending on the size of your pan, you may have to do this in batches.

Prepare the sauce
Heat the oil in a large karahi or wide saucepan on a medium heat and add the cumin seeds, allowing them to sizzle for a few seconds. Add the onions and fry for 5 minutes. Lower the heat slightly and fry for a further 8-10 minutes until soft and dark golden.

Add the ginger, garlic and chillies and stir for a minute. Add 100ml of the water and stir for five minutes before adding the turmeric, garam masala and salt. Stir briskly to prevent the spices from sticking to the bottom of the pan. Add another 100ml of water. Continue stirring for a further 5 minutes.

Add the tomatoes and cook on a medium heat for 10-12 minutes, stirring from time to time. It should just be cooking gently, allowing the sauce to become fairly thick. You'll know it's ready when the sauce is thick enough to slide off the sides of the pan. If the sauce does begin to stick, lower the heat and add a splash of water.

Complete the dish
Stir in the remaining 300ml of water and then lower the meatballs into the sauce. Cover the pan, leaving a small gap, and cook on a low heat for 15 minutes or until the meatballs are cooked through.

PRAWNS WITH SWEET RED PEPPERS

Sweet charred peppers and spicy prawns make for a combination that brings out the very best of European and Indian cooking. I tend to serve this dish cold with plenty of coconut and coriander chutney (page 204) and hot naan bread (page 186).

Serves 6

3 red bell peppers, halved lengthways, seeds removed and then cut into 1cm-wide strips
3 tbsp extra virgin olive oil
a pinch of sea salt flakes
1 tbsp cumin seeds
1 large onion, chopped
30g ginger, finely chopped

4 cloves garlic, finely chopped
2 red chillies, finely chopped
½ tsp salt
250g ripe tomatoes, finely chopped
750g peeled raw king prawns
a handful of coriander leaves, to garnish

Preheat the oven to 170°C/325°F/Gas Mark 3.

Spread the peppers out on a baking tray, drizzle lightly with 1 tbsp of the extra virgin olive oil, sprinkle over with the sea salt and toss to mix. Roast in the oven for 30-35 minutes, checking halfway through and giving the tray a shake to prevent the vegetables from sticking. They should be slightly charred to bring out their sweetness.

Heat the oil in a large karahi or frying pan on a medium heat and add the cumin seeds, allowing them to sizzle for a few seconds. Add the onions and cook for 2 minutes, then add the ginger, garlic and chillies. Stir for a further 2 minutes before adding the salt and tomatoes and then cook for another 2 minutes.

Lower in the prawns and cook for 2 minutes. Add the peppers, gently mixing everything together, and cook for a further minute or so until the prawns change colour and are cooked through. Garnish with the chopped coriander.

FISH KOFTAS

Though these fish balls look deceptively meek and mild after they have been poached, they actually pack a spicy punch, which is intensified by the rich sauce. The koftas can be prepared in advance, poached, and kept in the fridge until needed. Remove from the fridge 20-30 minutes before adding them to the sauce. Be careful when mincing the fish as you want it to retain its texture and not become a paste. Serve with rice (page 196), yogurt (page 222) and tomato and cucumber salad (page 206). *Photo page 86.*

Serves 6-8

For the fish balls
1kg skinless white fish fillets,
   (cod or haddock both work well),
   coarsely minced
1 small onion, finely chopped
30g ginger, finely chopped
2 green chillies, finely chopped
1 tsp garam masala
1 tsp salt
a handful of coriander leaves,
   finely chopped
2 slices bread, soaked in water for
   5 minutes, drained and squeezed
   of excess water
1 litre cold water, for poaching the
   fish balls

For the tomato sauce
4 tbsp oil
1 tbsp cumin seeds
2 medium onions, chopped
40g ginger, finely chopped
3 cloves garlic, finely chopped
2 green chillies, finely chopped
200ml freshly boiled water
1 tsp turmeric
1 tbsp garam masala
1 tsp salt
550g ripe tomatoes, blended
   or 400g passata

Prepare the fish balls
Put the minced fish in a large bowl. Add all the other ingredients, except the poaching water. Wet your hands a little and mix thoroughly. Form into balls about 5cm in diameter, being careful not to make them overly firm. Makes approximately 20 balls.

Bring the water to a simmer in a shallow pan. In batches, add the fish balls to the water and poach on a medium heat for 4-5 minutes, turning the balls halfway through to ensure even cooking. Remove with a slotted spoon. Cool and cover the fish balls and place in the fridge for at least 30 minutes to firm up. Retain the poaching water.

Prepare the tomato sauce
Heat the oil in a large karahi or sauté pan on a medium heat and add the cumin seeds, allowing them to sizzle for a few seconds. Add the onions and fry for 5 minutes. Lower the heat slightly and fry for a further 8-10 minutes until dark golden.

Add the ginger, garlic and chillies and stir thoroughly. Add 100ml of the boiled water and stir for a few minutes before adding the turmeric, garam masala and salt. Stir briskly to prevent the spices from sticking to the bottom of the pan. Add the remaining 100ml of hot water. Continue stirring for a further 5 minutes. Add the tomatoes and cook on a medium heat for 10-15 minutes, stirring from time to time. You should have a fairly thick sauce.

Complete the dish
Add the poaching water to the sauce and stir. Bring to the boil and then simmer for 2 minutes or so. The sauce will be quite thin. Lower in the fish balls, stirring gently until they are coated with the sauce. Cover with a lid and heat through for 3-4 minutes.

FISH IN A VINEGAR, FENUGREEK AND YOGURT SAUCE

This tangy sauce complements delicate white fish as it is less overpowering than some heavy, tomato-based curries. To be sure that it retains its flaky texture and flavour, be careful not to overcook the fish. You can either bake this dish in the oven or cook it in a large frying pan.

This is a really quick dish to prepare and cook, making it perfect for a post-work treat (although it's pretty good at the weekend, too). The fenugreek seeds are very strongly flavoured so don't go overboard with them.

Serves 6-8

3 tbsp oil
½ tsp fenugreek seeds
1 tbsp cumin seeds
2 medium onions, roughly chopped
40g ginger, finely chopped
5 cloves garlic, finely chopped
2 green chillies, finely chopped
1 tsp turmeric
1 tsp garam masala
1 tsp salt
50ml freshly boiled water

200g ripe tomatoes, blended or finely chopped
2 tbsp malt vinegar
500g natural yogurt
1.2kg skinless firm white fish fillets, (e.g. halibut, cod or haddock), cut into 6-8 pieces
a little oil to grease the oven dish, if baking
a handful of coriander leaves, chopped, to garnish

If baking, preheat the oven to 180°C/350°F/Gas Mark 4.

Heat the oil in a large karahi or deep-sided frying pan on a medium heat and add the fenugreek and cumin seeds, allowing them to sizzle for a few seconds. Add the onions and fry for 5 minutes until lightly golden. Add the ginger, garlic, chillies, turmeric, garam masala and salt and stir thoroughly. Add the water and stir for a few minutes. Add the tomatoes and vinegar and cook for 3-4 minutes. Add the yogurt a little at a time, stirring continuously (if you put the yogurt in too quickly, it has a tendency to curdle).

If cooking on the stovetop, add the fish to the pan. Cook for approximately 7-10 minutes or until done. Be careful to handle the fish carefully to prevent it breaking up. Alternatively, if baking, brush the oven dish with oil. Arrange the fish pieces slightly spaced apart and spoon the sauce over and around them. Cook for approximately 15 minutes or so, but keep a close eye on it. Garnish with the chopped coriander.

KERALAN-STYLE PRAWNS IN A TAMARIND AND COCONUT SAUCE

Our trip to Kerala was all the more memorable because we met up with our friend, Ruben, who grew up there. We stayed at his family home with his mother, where we feasted on lots of home cooking with spices from the garden that we would never be able to grow in England: black pepper, ginger, turmeric and tamarind. When we ate at the local restaurant, with its beautiful view of the sea, Ruben and Atul, my husband, could put in a special request for the fish they wanted to eat the following evening. For lovers of fish and seafood, this part of India is a true haven. The fish caught early in the morning is prepared and ready to be eaten within a few hours.

Here, cooking the prawns with their shells on keeps in the flavour and prevents them from getting overcooked and squidgy. Plus, it makes for more fun at the table watching your fellow diners peeling them!

For a vegetarian version, omit the prawns and use 3 sweetcorn cobs, each one cut into 3 pieces. Add to the pan when the coconut milk has come to the boil. Simmer for about 10 minutes or until the kernels are soft. *Photo page 92.*

Serves 6

2 tbsp tamarind concentrate, dissolved in 50ml cold water
3 tbsp oil
1 tbsp black mustard seeds
1 tsp fenugreek seeds
1 tsp cumin seeds
1 tbsp black peppercorns, lightly crushed
15 curry (neem) leaves, fresh or dried
1 medium onion, finely chopped
40g ginger, finely chopped

4 cloves garlic, finely chopped
4 red chillies, finely chopped
1 tbsp ground cumin
1 tsp turmeric
1 tsp salt
100ml freshly boiled water
250g ripe tomatoes, blended or 200g passata
800ml coconut milk
800g raw shell-on jumbo king prawns or 750g raw peeled jumbo king prawns

Heat the oil in a large karahi or saucepan on a medium heat until it is smoking ever so slightly. Add the mustard seeds, cover with a lid until they start popping and then add the fenugreek seeds, cumin seeds, crushed peppercorns and neem leaves, allowing them to sizzle for just a few seconds.

Add the onions and fry for 4-5 minutes. Lower the heat slightly and add the ginger, garlic, chillies, ground cumin, turmeric and salt. Stir for 3-4 minutes and then add the 100ml of water. Continue stirring for another 4-5 minutes. Add the tomatoes and cook for 6-8 minutes more until you have a fairly thick sauce.

Pour in the coconut milk and add the tamarind water. Bring to the boil and then simmer for 7-8 minutes until slightly thickened. Lower in the prawns and heat for 2-3 minutes until they change colour and are cooked through. Serve with plain rice (page 196) and okra (page 142).

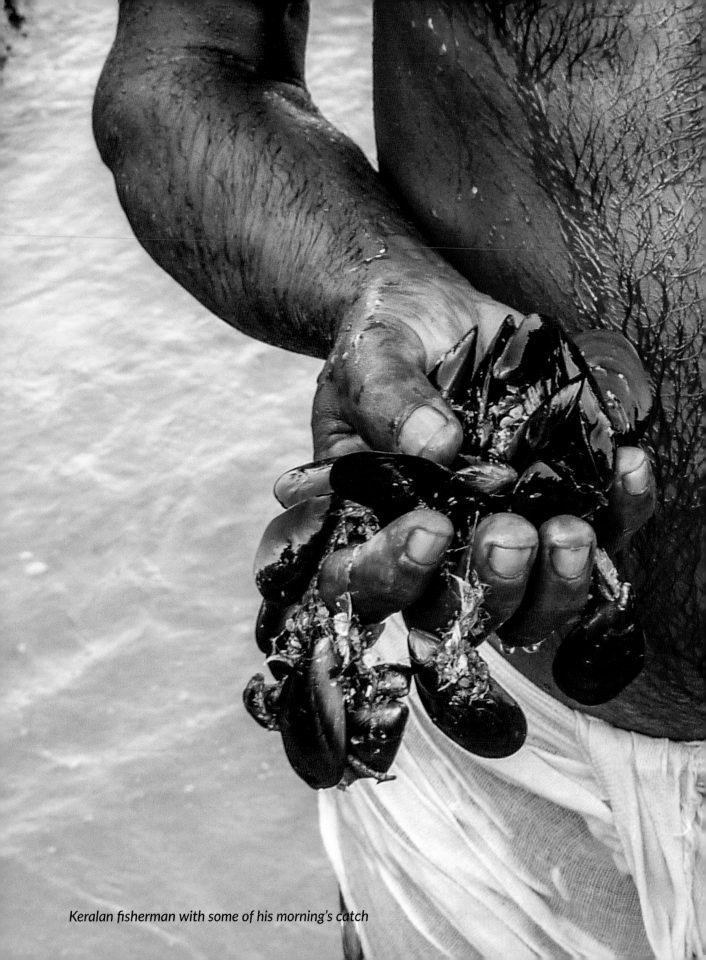

Keralan fisherman with some of his morning's catch

Peppercorns drying in the afternoon sun in Kerala.

PULSES

MUNG DAL YELLOW

MUNG DAL YELLOW

MUNG DAL YELLOW

MUNG DAL YELLOW

MUNG DAL YELLOW

MUNG DAL YELLOW

Moong Dall Washed 500g℮

MUNG DAL YELLOW

MUNG DAL
YELLOW

Quick midweek suppers and hearty weekend recipes

Beans, lentils and peas have a very special place in Indian cuisine. For vegetarians like me, they are an important source of protein and I see them as the essence of home cooking. These would rival any meat dish in terms of depth of flavour and they're also very healthy, of course. You will always find a great variety of dhals in an Indian home, usually stored in great big sweet jars – they are that popular.

There are various techniques to cook pulses and you can mix and match them; each one is worth trying.

The easiest method is to throw all the ingredients into the pot and boil them all together. Alternatively, you can cook the pulses on their own until tender and then combine them with a masala (onion and tomato sauce). The last method is to prepare a tarka separately by gently frying cumin seeds, fresh ginger, garlic and chilli and then adding them to the cooked lentils. This is best done just before serving when the tarka is fresh and can impart all its flavours and aromas to the dish.

Some dried pulses will need soaking well in advance so, if you're using them and don't want to be caught out, check the recipe beforehand. Remember too that they will thicken as they cool, and this will affect the final consistency.

There are a great many pulses available in Asian shops: from oily or creamy, to big and chunky, or small and flat. So have some fun by experimenting with them using these recipes.

MASOORA DI DHAL
Red split lentils

Back in the 80s, I was lucky enough to be travelling in China with my husband for two months. Having survived on a backpacker's budget for the entire trip, we were desperate (really desperate!) for some Indian food on our return to the UK. This dhal – quick, light and easy – was what my mum cooked for us as soon as we walked through the door and it was one of the most welcoming and fulfilling meals I have ever eaten. Serve with chapati (page 182), yogurt (page 222) and lemon and ginger pickle (page 210). Yummy.

You can also prepare mungi di dhal (yellow split mung beans) using exactly the same ingredients and method.

Serves 6

For the dhal
300g red split lentils,
   rinsed and drained
2 medium onions, finely chopped
2 tsp ground turmeric
1 tbsp garam masala
1 tsp salt
800g ripe tomatoes, blended
  or 600g passata
1 litre cold water

For the tarka
3 tbsp oil
1 tbsp cumin seeds
80g ginger, finely chopped
6 cloves garlic, finely chopped
2 green chillies, finely chopped

Prepare the dhal
Put all the dhal ingredients into a large heavy-based saucepan. Bring to the boil and then cover and cook on a low heat for a further 15-20 minutes or so until the lentils are soft. Don't forget to stir occasionally to stop the lentils sticking to the bottom of the pan.

Prepare the tarka
Heat the oil in a small frying pan on a medium heat and add the cumin seeds, allowing them to sizzle for a few seconds. Lower the heat, add the ginger, garlic and chillies, and fry for about 3-4 minutes until a light golden colour. Don't cook it too quickly, as it will taste raw – and don't burn it, as it will taste bitter.

Stir the tarka into the dhal and serve.

KABULI SHOLAY

Chickpeas in an onion and tomato sauce

To prepare this recipe, I favour a more traditional approach using dried chickpeas (soaked overnight) because I prefer their creamier texture. That said, using tinned chickpeas will give you very similar results and enable you to skip the first few steps and go straight to heating the oil. Serve hot as a main course with rice (page 196) or pooris (page 190), or as a side dish – topped with chopped tomatoes and, if you like, some tamarind (page 214) drizzled over.

Use an extra-large bowl if soaking the chickpeas as they will double in size when they absorb the water.

Rawan (black-eyed beans) can be prepared similarly to chickpeas. Use the same ingredients but omit the mango powder. If you're cooking them in the traditional way and using dried beans, boil vigorously for 15 minutes and then with the lid on for 30-40 minutes.
Photo page 106.

Serves 6-8

For the chickpeas
400g dried chickpeas, rinsed and
   soaked in 2 litres of cold water
   for 8-12 hours (or overnight)
2.5 litres cold water for cooking
   the chickpeas
or
3x 400g tins of chickpeas,
   drained and rinsed
   (about 720g drained weight)

For the sauce
4 tbsp oil
1 tbsp cumin seeds
1 cinnamon stick, about 5cm
2 black cardamom pods
2 medium onions, finely chopped
100g ginger, finely chopped
4 cloves garlic, finely chopped
2 green chillies, finely chopped
1 tsp ground turmeric
1 tsp ground black pepper
1 tsp mango powder (optional)
1 tbsp garam masala
1 tsp salt
100ml freshly boiled water,
   if using tinned chickpeas
350g ripe tomatoes, blended
   or 300g passata

Prepare the chickpeas

If using tinned chickpeas, skip this first paragraph and start below. If using dried chickpeas, rinse them after soaking and put into a large saucepan. Add the 2.5 litres of cold water, bring to the boil and continue boiling vigorously for 20 minutes, skimming off any froth. Cover the pan completely and cook on a medium heat for an hour or more until soft, stirring from time to time. Drain the chickpeas, reserving the cooking water for later. Set aside.

Prepare the sauce

Heat the oil in a large karahi or heavy-based saucepan on a medium heat and add the cumin seeds, cinnamon stick and cardamom, allowing them to sizzle for a few seconds. Add the onions and fry for 5 minutes. Lower the heat slightly and fry for a further 4-5 minutes. The onions should be soft and golden.

Turn the heat right down, add the ginger, garlic and chillies, and stir briskly for a few minutes. Add the turmeric, black pepper, mango powder, garam masala and salt. When the spices are completely absorbed into the mixture, add 50ml of the hot water and stir for a few minutes. When the water has evaporated, add the remaining water. Continue stirring for a further 3-4 minutes. Don't rush this stage as the ingredients should be cooked thoroughly and not taste raw. This is what will give your finished dish its depth of flavour.

Add the tomatoes and cook gently for 10-15 minutes, stirring from time to time, until the sauce becomes fairly thick. You'll know it's ready when the sauce is a rich reddish-brown and thick enough to slide slowly off the sides of the pan.

Complete the dish

Add the chickpeas and cook on a low heat for 10 minutes. If you prefer, you can decrease the thickness of the sauce by gradually adding a few ladlefuls of the reserved water or, if using tinned chickpeas, add the freshly boiled water. Cook for a further 10 minutes to allow the sauce to thicken a little.

RAJMAH
Red kidney beans

These beautiful burgundy-coloured beans have a deep, rounded, earthy flavour. When my parents first came to England, they didn't have central heating and we relied on coal fires and rich comforting dishes like this to keep us warm in what seemed like never-ending winters. I vividly remember newspaper spread over the carpet and meals served on trays and eaten cross-legged in front of the fire. As was the case then, I still think this is best served with chapati (page 182) or piping hot rice (page 196).

Use an extra-large bowl to soak the dried kidney beans, as they will double in size when they absorb the water.

Serves 6

400g dried red kidney beans, rinsed and soaked in 2 litres of cold water for 8-12 hours (or overnight)
1 large onion, very finely chopped
50g ginger, very finely chopped
6 cloves garlic, very finely chopped
2 green chillies, finely chopped

1 tsp turmeric
1 tbsp garam masala
1 tsp salt
1 cinnamon stick, about 5cm
2 black cardamom pods
250g ripe tomatoes, blended or 200g passata
1 tbsp tomato puree
2 litres cold water

Rinse and drain the pre-soaked beans.

Put all the ingredients into a large heavy-based saucepan. Bring to the boil and continue boiling vigorously for 15 minutes. Lower the heat, cover and simmer for about an hour and a half or so until the beans are completely soft, stirring from time to time. Add more water if the sauce seems too dry; it should have the consistency of a thick soup. If it's too runny, simply take a ladleful of beans from the pan and mash them before returning to the pot, stirring in well.

MAH DI DHAL
Whole urid (whole black gram)

This dhal is known to Indians as dhal makhani (black dhal with butter) and is a typical farmer's lunch, packing enough sustenance to keep them going through the whole day. For us non-farming types, it's a luxurious, velvety dish and one of my favourite dhals. In India, and even in many Indian restaurants here in the UK and abroad, this dhal seems to have a wonderful smokiness to it – an effect that is easier than you may think to achieve at home, provided you don't mind using a lump of hot charcoal in the kitchen. And it's absolutely worth it.

Even if you decide not to go down the smoked route, just add a blob of butter when serving to give it a rich creamy finish.

You can make this dhal without the kidney beans, in which case you'll need to increase the amount of whole gram. If you are cooking with the dried kidney beans, use an extra-large bowl to soak them, as they will double in size when they absorb the water. *Photo page 112.*

Serves 6

1 x 400g tin of red kidney beans
or
150g dried red kidney beans,
   rinsed and soaked in 1.5 litres of
   cold water for 8-12 hours
   (or overnight)
300g whole black gram (or 400g if
   omitting the kidney beans),
   rinsed and drained
2 medium onions, finely chopped
100g ginger, finely chopped
8 cloves garlic, finely chopped
4 green chillies, finely chopped

1 tbsp cumin seeds
1 tbsp turmeric
1 tbsp garam masala
1½ tsp salt
2 black cardamom pods
1 cinnamon stick, about 5cm
400g ripe tomatoes, blended
   or 300g passata
2 tbsp tomato puree
3 litres cold water
40-50ml ghee or 40ml oil, for
   the optional smoking
60g butter or ghee, to serve

If using tinned kidney beans, you don't need to do anything with them until the dhal is cooked. Alternatively, if using dried kidney beans, rinse them after soaking and put into a large heavy-bottomed saucepan. Add all the ingredients, except the ghee, oil and butter. Bring to the boil and continue boiling vigorously for 15 minutes. Cover, lower the heat and cook for about three and a half hours or more. Stir, stir, and stir again, as the dhal thickens. If it is beginning to stick, add a little extra water. When cooked, the dhal will be a deep, dark brown and the lentils soft. If using tinned kidney beans, add them a few minutes before the end of the cooking time.

To add that extra special touch, use the following charcoal technique... Heat a thick piece of charcoal over an open flame for about 15 minutes, turning once or twice with metal tongs. Then place a small heatproof bowl directly on top of the dhal, carefully put the hot charcoal into it and immediately pour the ghee or oil onto the coal. This will produce a lot of smoke, which you want to lock into the dish as soon as possible with a tight fitting lid. Leave the pot to stand for 2-3 minutes, take off the lid, remove the bowl and give the pan a good stir. Your dhal should now have a lovely, smoky note to it.

Add the butter or ghee, give it another good stir, and serve.

CHANA DHAL
Yellow split chickpeas

This wholesome nutty dhal can be enjoyed with aubergines with potatoes (page 146) or spinach with potatoes (page 122). I always serve it with fresh green chillies and lemon and ginger pickle (page 210) on the side.

When you buy this dhal, don't confuse yellow split peas with yellow split chickpeas. They look similar but the lentils for this dish are slightly wrinkled, whereas split peas are smoother.

You can also prepare sabut masoor (brown lentils) using exactly the same ingredients and method.

Serves 6

For the dhal
300g yellow split chickpeas,
   rinsed in cold water
2 medium onions, finely chopped
1 tsp ground turmeric
1 tbsp garam masala
1 tsp salt
650g ripe tomatoes, blended
   or 500g passata
1.5 litres cold water

For the tarka
4 tbsp oil
1 tbsp cumin seeds
80g ginger, finely chopped
6 cloves garlic, finely chopped
2 green chillies, finely chopped

Prepare the dhal
Put all the dhal ingredients into a large heavy-based saucepan. Bring to the boil and continue boiling vigorously for 5 minutes. Cover and cook on a low heat for about an hour or until the lentils are soft but still retain their shape. Don't forget to stir, particularly towards the end of the cooking time when the lentils will have thickened considerably. If the dhal begins to stick, add a little extra water.

Prepare the tarka
Heat the oil in a small frying pan on a medium heat and add the cumin seeds, allowing them to sizzle for a few seconds. Add the ginger, garlic and chillies and fry gently on a really low heat for about 3-4 minutes until a light golden colour. Don't cook it too quickly, as it will taste raw – and don't burn it, as it will taste bitter.

Stir the tarka into the dhal and serve.

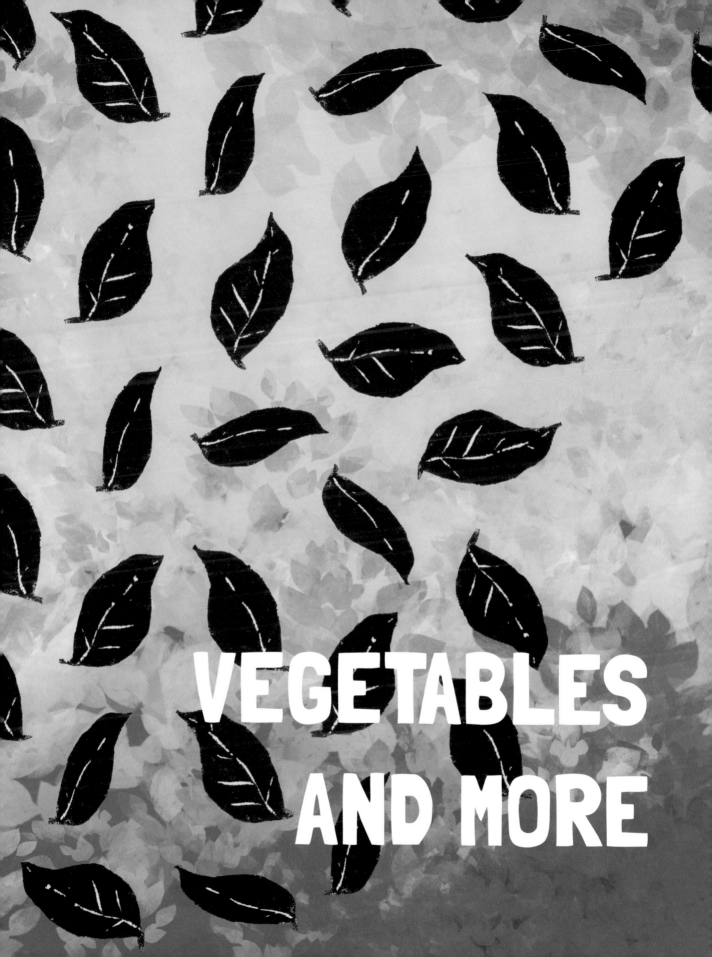

VEGETABLES
AND MORE

Fresh colourful sides and mouth-watering mains

If you ever get the opportunity to travel to India, you will find that it is a vegetarian's wonderland. Where else in the world is the selection of vegetarian dishes wide enough to rival or even outdo the choice of meat-based dishes? This is true for home cooking and restaurants, as well as for the famous street food stalls.

Ordinary vegetables like potatoes, cauliflower or cabbage are made so much more interesting through simple cooking techniques and the addition of a few spices. My favourites are the more unusual and exotic vegetables like okra and aubergine. In my experience, people shy away from them, but this could be because they are unfamiliar with how to cook them.

In this section I have also included paneer, which is an Indian type of unaged cheese, and is a familiar part of Indian vegetarian cuisine. Its texture resembles that of feta cheese. It is typically pressed into a cube or used crumbled. Its mild yet creamy flavour easily combines with rich spices to make it really versatile. It can be fried, it can be barbecued, or it can accompany vegetables such as spinach, peppers and peas. See also Glossary (pages 257-258).

You will find that a great many Punjabi-style recipes begin by making a masala (not to be confused with the type of masala that is a blend of spices e.g. garam masala). The ingredients – cumin seeds, onion, ginger, garlic, chilli and tomato – are always the same and are used to prepare a thick sauce. You can add almost any vegetable to this basic sauce.

Follow these recipes and you'll become an expert in producing a huge variety of dishes, from the earthy flavours of okra to the summery, sweet, fresh flavours of carrots, beans and courgettes. I dare you to be adventurous and experiment with your own combinations of vegetables.

ALOO PALAK
Potatoes with spinach

Spinach is a popular vegetable in the Punjab. My mum still grows it all year round and makes sure that I do, too. Normal spinach is more robust than the baby variety, but it's also a little more bitter. Try different types and see which you prefer. Whichever variety you choose, it will require only minimal cooking, so watch it closely.

Serves 6

3 tbsp oil
2 tsp cumin seeds
1 small onion, roughly chopped
25g ginger, finely chopped
2 cloves garlic, finely chopped
2 green chillies, finely chopped
1 tsp ground turmeric
½ tsp garam masala

¾ tsp salt
450g ripe tomatoes, blended
  or 350g passata
350g all-purpose potatoes,
  peeled and cut into 1.5cm cubes
600g spinach leaves,
  quite finely chopped

Heat the oil in a large karahi or saucepan on a medium heat and add the cumin seeds, allowing them to sizzle for a few seconds. Add the onions and fry for 5-6 minutes until soft and lightly golden. Then add the ginger, garlic, chillies, turmeric, garam masala and salt. Stir briskly for 2-3 minutes, adding a splash of water if the mixture begins to stick to the bottom of the pan. Now add the tomatoes and potatoes. Turn the heat to low, cover and cook for 6-8 minutes until just over half-cooked.

Put the spinach on top of the potatoes and cover for a minute to allow the leaves to wilt just a little. Take the lid off and stir gently. Cover again and cook for a further 6-8 minutes on a low heat until the spinach has completely wilted and the potatoes are soft.

ROASTED AUBERGINES AND RED PEPPERS WITH SWEET AND SOUR TAMARIND

The distinctive flavour of aubergine can vary greatly depending on how it is cooked and the ingredients that it is combined with. Here, mixing the aubergines and peppers with tamarind brings a tart sweetness. Simple to make and scrumptious to eat!

Serve hot or cold, as a salad or as an accompaniment to a main course. As with the other aubergine recipes, I prefer to salt the aubergines to get rid of any bitterness but if you are using the smaller Indian type, you can leave out the first step.

Serves 6

600g small aubergines, quartered lengthways or 600g large aubergines quartered lengthways, then cut crossways into 1.5cm-thick chunks plus 1 tsp salt, to sprinkle over the aubergines

3 red bell peppers, halved lengthways, seeds removed and then cut into 1cm-wide strips
6 tbsp extra virgin olive oil
1 medium red onion, not too thinly sliced
2 tbsp *tamarind chutney* (page 214)
a handful of coriander leaves, chopped, to garnish

Put the aubergine pieces into a colander, sprinkle the teaspoon of salt over them and leave to drain for 30 minutes. Using kitchen paper or a tea towel, gently squeeze out the excess moisture from the aubergines. Set aside.

Preheat the oven to 180°C/350°F/Gas Mark 4.

Put the aubergines on a baking tray and toss lightly with 2 tbsp of the oil. Using another 2 tbsp of oil, do the same for the peppers on a separate baking tray. Make sure the vegetables are spread out as a single layer because you want them to be roasted rather than steamed. Depending on the size of your oven and trays, you may have to do this in batches.

Place the trays in the oven and roast for 20-25 minutes, checking halfway through and giving the trays a bit of a shake to prevent the vegetables from sticking. The peppers should be slightly charred and the aubergines golden.

Heat the remaining 2 tbsp of oil in a large karahi or sauté pan and gently fry the onions for about 3-4 minutes. Turn off the heat. Add the roasted vegetables to the pan and pour the tamarind chutney over them. Transfer to a shallow serving dish. Garnish with the coriander.

GREEN BEANS WITH MUSTARD SEEDS

The easiest and quickest recipe in this book. The beans are simply tossed in hot oil, sautéed with the nutty flavour of the mustard seeds, and then finished with a sprinkling of salt flakes. I prefer beans to retain some of their freshly picked crunchiness, so I don't bother to blanch them. It's a lovely, light side dish to go with the other, heavier mains. Serve hot or cold.

Serves 6

2 tbsp oil
1 tbsp black mustard seeds
600g green beans, stalks trimmed
¾ tsp sea salt flakes

Heat the oil in a medium-sized karahi or deep-sided frying pan on a medium heat. Add the mustard seeds, cover with a lid until they start popping and then add the beans and salt, stirring for 2-4 minutes depending on the texture you prefer.

BARBECUED PANEER

Barbecues are often heavily geared towards meat eaters. Vegetarians are frequently left with just a selection of side-salads and bread. Perhaps this spicy and satisfying barbecued cheese recipe can help change that. It uses the same ingredients as the barbecued chicken recipe, with the addition of lime at the end to counter the natural saltiness of the cheese. As it needs to be threaded onto skewers, I tend to use shop-bought paneer as it is much firmer and less likely to fall apart.

Serves 6

150g natural yogurt
30g ginger, finely chopped
3 cloves garlic, finely chopped
½ tsp chilli flakes
1 tsp ground black pepper
3 tsp ground cumin

1 tsp paprika
1 tsp salt
500g paneer, cut into 2cm cubes
a little oil, to brush over
   the skewers
1 lime, cut into wedges

Put the yogurt into a large bowl and stir in all the spices. Add the paneer and coat it with the yogurt. Leave to marinate for 15 minutes.

Brush the skewers lightly with oil. Thread the paneer onto the skewers so that the cubes are not quite touching. This will help it to cook evenly.

Preheat your barbecue to a medium heat. Grill for about a minute on each side or until lightly golden. Serve immediately, with the lime wedges on the side.

VEGETABLE BIRYANI

This vegetarian version of a biryani shares all the features that make the meat dish so good. The spices, saffron-infused rice, crispy onions, coriander and mint are the same in both recipes. Here though, it is the medley of crunchy vegetables with their vibrant colours that are the true gems. Wait until your guests are comfortably seated and then... present with gusto. Serve with raita (page 224).

As with the chicken biryani, make it easier for yourself by measuring out the ingredients beforehand. If cooking on the stovetop, place the pan on a heat diffuser (see page 267) or cast-iron frying pan so that the vegetables and rice cook slowly and evenly. *Photo page 132.*

Serves 6

For the vegetables
4 tbsp oil
1 tbsp cumin seeds
1 tsp black peppercorns
5 cloves
1 black cardamom pod
1 cinnamon stick, about 5cm
1 bay leaf
200g carrots, cut into 1cm cubes
200g cauliflower, cut into small florets
200g green beans, stalks trimmed and cut into 2cm pieces
1 large red bell pepper, halved lengthways, seeds removed and diced into 2cm pieces
1 tbsp ground cumin
1 tbsp ground coriander
½ tsp turmeric
1 tsp salt
40g ginger, finely chopped
3 cloves garlic, finely chopped
2 green chillies, finely chopped
100g ripe tomatoes, blended or 80g passata
150g natural yogurt

For the onions
150ml oil
3 medium onions, finely sliced

For the rice
300g basmati rice, rinsed and soaked in cold water for 30 minutes
1 tsp cumin seeds
2 black cardamom pods
2 green cardamom pods
1 cinnamon stick, about 5cm
2 bay leaves
1 tsp salt
800ml cold water

To assemble the dish
a knob of butter, to grease the pan
a generous pinch of saffron strands, soaked in 4 tbsp hot milk
a handful of mint leaves, roughly chopped
a handful of coriander leaves, roughly chopped
5 x 1 tsp unsalted butter

Prepare the vegetables
Heat the oil in a large karahi or wide-bottomed saucepan on a medium heat and add the cumin seeds, peppercorns, cloves, cardamom, cinnamon and bay leaf, allowing them to sizzle for a few seconds.

Add the carrots, cauliflower, beans and peppers and stir-fry for about 30 seconds. Add the ground cumin, coriander, turmeric and salt, followed by the ginger, garlic and chillies. Stir, so that the spices coat the vegetables. Add the tomatoes and yogurt and continue stirring for a further minute. Set aside.

Prepare the onion
Heat the oil in a large karahi or deep-sided frying pan on a medium heat. Add the onions and fry for about 10-15 minutes, stirring so that they do not stick to the pan. When done, they should be soft in the middle and dark golden brown on the outside (but not burnt).

Remove from the heat with a slotted spoon and spread out on kitchen paper. Take some more kitchen paper and press down on the onions to remove any excess oil. As they cool, they will become crispy. Set aside.

Prepare the rice
Drain the rice and put in a large pan with the spices. Add the water and bring to the boil, then simmer for 4-5 minutes. The rice should be only partially cooked, soft on the outside and still firm in the middle, as it will cook fully later. Remove from the heat and drain any excess water.

Assemble the dish
If cooking in the oven, preheat to 180°C/350°F/Gas Mark 4.

Generously butter a large heavy-based saucepan or ovenproof dish that has a tight-fitting lid. Arrange the vegetables evenly on the bottom. Spread half of the fried onions over the vegetables and sprinkle the mint and coriander leaves on top, followed by half of the rice. Drizzle half of the saffron milk over. Add the other half of the rice, followed by a final sprinkle of the saffron milk. Finish by dotting the small knobs of butter on top.

Cover the dish with baking parchment (or foil) before placing the lid on, as you want to retain as much steam as possible to ensure it all cooks properly. If cooking on the hob, place the pan on a heat diffuser on a very low heat for 35-40 minutes, by which time your rice and vegetables should be done. Alternatively, place in the oven and cook for 40-50 minutes. Leave to stand for 10 minutes before removing the lid. Spoon onto a serving platter and garnish with the remaining crispy onions.

INDIAN OMELETTE

Quick and easy, this fluffy omelette is ideal to serve for brunch. The coriander retains its fresh lemony taste, as cooking time is so short. For something different, try it with hot buttered toast, smoked salmon and lemon and ginger pickle (page 210). There are a few ways to finish off cooking the omelette: folding it French style, flipping it in the Indian way or simply popping it under a hot grill until golden.

Match your frying pan to the number of eggs you're using – too big and the omelette will be papery, too small and it will be overcooked on the outside and runny on the inside.

Serves 2

4-5 large eggs
2 tsp cumin seeds
½ small onion, roughly chopped
1 or 2 green chillies,
    roughly chopped
½ tsp ground black pepper

½ tsp garam masala (optional)
¼ tsp salt
a handful of coriander leaves,
    chopped
1 tbsp oil

If grilling, preheat the grill to medium.

Break the eggs into a bowl and lightly mix with a fork or whisk. Stir in the cumin seeds, onions, chillies, black pepper, garam masala, salt and coriander.

Heat the oil in a frying pan on a medium heat. Pour in the egg mixture to cover the bottom of the pan, and use a spatula to bring it in from the sides towards the centre of the pan as it cooks. Continue to heat until the egg is cooked through underneath but still runny on top. At this point, if you prefer a runnier omelette, fold it in half, cook a little longer and serve. Alternatively, flip it over completely to cook the underside, or place under a hot grill until lightly golden on top.

STUFFED PEPPERS

Spiced mashed potato is a wonderful thing, especially with the addition of tart mango powder. Here, it makes for a real standout dish with the vibrant colours of the peppers, sweetened after almost an hour in the oven. Serve with fresh, cool raita (page 224).

Serves 6

600g all-purpose potatoes, boiled and mashed
6 bell peppers – a selection of colours; tops, seeds and pith removed carefully
a little oil, to brush over the peppers
4 tbsp extra virgin olive oil
1 large onion, finely chopped

¼ tsp turmeric powder
1 tsp ground coriander
1 tsp ground black pepper
1½ tsp mango powder
1 tbsp garam masala
2 green chillies, finely chopped
a handful of coriander leaves, roughly chopped
½ tsp salt

Preheat the oven to 200°C/400°F/Gas Mark 6.

Brush the peppers with oil and put on a baking tray, cut-side up, and roast for 15-20 minutes.

In the meantime, heat the 4 tbsp of oil in a karahi or saucepan on a medium heat. Add the onions and fry for 5-7 minutes until lightly browned. Add the turmeric, ground coriander, black pepper, mango powder, garam masala, chillies and salt, and fry for a couple of minutes. Sprinkle in a little water if the mixture is beginning to stick to the pan. Add the potatoes and coriander and stir briskly for a few minutes, making sure that the onions are evenly dispersed and not all stuck together. Allow to cool.

Spoon the potato filling into the peppers and return to the oven. Bake for 50 minutes, a bit longer if you want the skin of the peppers to be really soft and slightly charred.

PALAK PANEER

Paneer with spinach

The rich subtle creaminess of the paneer is perfectly balanced with the bold flavour of the spinach. Don't be alarmed by the amount of spinach: it will reduce dramatically when cooked and the paneer remains the star of the show. This dish is a wonderful accompaniment to many meals, especially those with strong and distinctive flavours (e.g. spicy lamb, page 74) but it also offers a contrast to some of the lighter dishes (e.g. red lentils, page 102).

Serves 6

Approximately 250-300g
  paneer cubes (pages 257-8)
3 tbsp oil
1 large onion, chopped
20g ginger, finely chopped
2 cloves garlic, finely chopped
2 green chillies, finely chopped
1 tsp turmeric

1 tsp garam masala
1 tsp salt
450g ripe tomatoes, blended
  or 350g passata
600g spinach leaves,
  quite finely chopped
100ml freshly boiled water

Heat the oil in a large karahi or wide-bottomed saucepan on a medium heat. Add the onions and fry for 7-10 minutes until soft and lightly browned. Lower the heat and add the ginger, garlic, chillies, turmeric, garam masala and salt. Stir briskly for 3-4 minutes, adding a splash of water if necessary, so the spices do not stick to the pan. Add the tomatoes and cook for 5-7 minutes, or until the sauce is almost thick but still retains a little moisture.

Add the spinach and the hot water. Cover for 3-4 minutes until the spinach has just wilted a little. Stir and then put the cubes of paneer on top of the spinach and replace the lid. Cook for another few minutes until the spinach has completely wilted and the paneer is hot. Give it a gentle stir before serving.

KADHI
Sour yogurt sauce with potato fritters

I'd never attempted to make kadhi before writing this book. I always felt that it would be impossible to replicate my mum's delicious version. Even so, I knew for certain that most of my friends would never have tasted it before. Once I'd made up my mind to cook it, I phoned my mum for the recipe and she gave me a rough idea of the quantities I should be using. After several weeks of fine-tuning, I presented it to my parents. My mum found the sauce tasty, but a bit too thick. So back to the kitchen I went – and here it is!

This sauce is traditionally served with crispy potato fritters (page 24). Alternatively, simply add 125g of chopped spinach a few minutes before the end of the cooking time. Serve with rice (page 196) or chapati (page 182).

Serves 6

60g gram flour (besan), sieved
200g natural sour yogurt
    or 200g natural yogurt and
    the juice of 2 lemons
1 tbsp turmeric
1 litre cold water
3 tbsp oil
1 tbsp cumin seeds
1 tbsp coriander seeds,
    coarsely crushed

15 curry (neem) leaves,
    fresh or dried
1 medium onion, sliced
60g ginger, finely chopped
4 cloves garlic, finely chopped
4 green chillies, finely chopped
1 tsp salt
500ml freshly boiled water
1 tbsp garam masala
a half quantity of *potato fritters*
    (page 24)

In a very large bowl, whisk together the flour, yogurt (and lemon, if using), turmeric and cold water. Smooth out any lumps in the mixture and set aside.

Heat the oil in a large karahi or saucepan on a medium heat and add the cumin seeds, crushed coriander and curry leaves, allowing them to sizzle for a few seconds. Add the onions and fry for 6-7 minutes until lightly brown. Then add the ginger, garlic, chillies and salt. Stir briskly for 2-3 minutes.

Add the flour mixture and bring to a simmer. Cook for about 15 minutes, stirring frequently until slightly thickened. If it starts spitting, lower the heat – it should just be bubbling away gently. Add the 500ml of water and continue cooking on a low heat for 30 minutes. Add the garam masala, then cover and cook for a further 15 minutes.

Lower in the potato fritters, heat through for a couple of minutes and then serve immediately.

BHINDI
Okra with onion and tomato

Exotic and irresistible, the flavour of okra is very difficult to describe. If you like aubergine, asparagus or green peppers, there is a good chance that you will enjoy okra – or 'lady's fingers' as it is sometimes called. Here, mingled with the sweet flavours of onion and tomato, this often overlooked vegetable becomes inviting for even the most unadventurous of eaters, so give it a go – serve with meat, fish or a dhal with yogurt (page 222) on the side.

If okra is bendy and dull, it will be chewy (and possibly slimy) when cooked. Over-mature, it will be tough and fibrous. So for this recipe, it's important to use young, fresh okra. Look for a vibrant green colour with pods that snap cleanly in two.

Serves 6

4 tbsp oil
1 tbsp cumin seeds
1 large onion, chopped
1 tsp turmeric
1 tsp garam masala

1 tsp salt
350g ripe tomatoes, blended
  or 250g passata
600g okra, stalks trimmed, cut
  crossways into 1cm pieces

Heat the oil in a large karahi or sauté pan on a medium heat and add the cumin seeds, allowing them to sizzle for a few seconds. Add the onions and fry for 6-8 minutes until soft and golden. Then add the turmeric, garam masala and salt, and fry for 2 minutes. Add the tomatoes and cook for 7-8 minutes, stirring occasionally. It should just be cooking gently, allowing the sauce to thicken a little.

Add the okra and stir carefully. Then cover and cook for 6-8 minutes on a very low heat until just tender. Halfway through the cooking time, give the pan a little shake to prevent the okra from sticking to the bottom.

ALOO GOBI
Cauliflower with potatoes

Those who are regulars at their local Indian restaurant are probably familiar with this dish. For me, aloo gobi was one of the first dishes I learnt to cook as a youngster. In the school holidays, if my mum was at work, my younger brother and I would surprise her by doing the household chores. Being the older sister, I would delegate him to vacuum and mop while I prepared dinner. This was one of the easiest dishes I knew, so it almost always made its way onto the menu. I have changed it a little to make it even simpler to cook. The main thing to bear in mind is to avoid cutting the florets too small – it's best if they contain a bit of crunch.

Serves 6

2 tbsp oil
1 tbsp cumin seeds
½ tsp turmeric
1 tsp salt
550g ripe tomatoes, blended
   or 400g passata

300g all-purpose potatoes,
   peeled and cut into 2cm cubes
1 medium cauliflower, washed and
   cut into medium-sized florets;
   retain a handful of the
   outer leaves
3 whole green chillies
1 tbsp garam masala

Heat the oil in a large karahi or sauté pan on a medium heat and add the cumin seeds, allowing them to sizzle for a few seconds. Add the turmeric, salt, tomatoes and potatoes. Stir, cover and cook for 5 minutes.

Add the cauliflower and chillies, and stir gently, making sure the vegetables are coated with the sauce. Chop the leaves and stir in. Cover the pan again and cook on a low heat for a further 15-20 minutes or until the vegetables are cooked, stirring once halfway through. Sprinkle the garam masala over at the end of the cooking time and give it another careful stir.

ALOO BAINGAN
Aubergine with potato

Like many kids, I didn't really like aubergines in my childhood. Over the years, though, I have grown to love their distinctive taste and versatility. The large purple variety may need to be salted to get rid of any bitterness, as in the aubergine and red pepper recipe (page 124). However, if you are using the smaller, less bitter, Indian type you can leave out the first step. The earthy texture of this dish makes a great contrast with the light, sharp flavour of the tomato and onion salad (page 212). Serve simply with chapati (page 182) or for something more special, poori (deep-fried bread, page 190).

Serves 6

600g small aubergines, quartered lengthways or 600g large aubergines, quartered lengthways, then cut crossways into 1.5cm thick chunks plus 1 tsp salt, to sprinkle over the aubergines
3 tbsp oil
1 tbsp cumin seeds
1 large onion, roughly chopped
30g ginger, finely chopped

3 cloves garlic, finely chopped
2 green chillies, finely chopped
½ tsp turmeric
1 tbsp garam masala
½ tsp salt
25ml freshly boiled water
400g ripe tomatoes, blended or 300g passata
200g all-purpose potatoes, peeled and cut into 2.5cm cubes

If using the large variety of aubergine put the chunks into a colander, sprinkle the teaspoon of salt over and leave to drain for 30 minutes. Using kitchen paper or a tea towel, gently squeeze out the excess moisture from the aubergines. Set aside.

Heat the oil in a large karahi or sauté pan on a medium heat and add the cumin seeds, allowing them to sizzle for a few seconds. Add the onions and fry for 3-4 minutes. Then add the ginger, garlic, chillies, turmeric, garam masala and salt, and stir thoroughly. Now add the water and stir for a few minutes.

Add the tomatoes and potatoes, cover and cook for 4-5 minutes. The potatoes should be about half done. Then add the aubergines, cover and cook for 12-15 minutes or until all the vegetables are done, adding a splash of water if they start sticking to the pan. Avoid taking the lid off, as you want the vegetables to cook in their own steam. Just give the pan a little shake every now and then to move them around.

MATAR PANEER
Paneer with peas

I remember having this dish for the first time when we were visiting my mum's best friend, Aunty Sagoo. This was where my younger brother and I spent much of our summer holidays. On my aunt's day off from work, we children would go off and play at the local park knowing that, on our return, we would be enjoying something really tasty. This dish was a firm favourite. The rich creamy flavour of the paneer is offset with the simple addition of peas, whose fresh, subtle sweetness creates something rather special. You can buy paneer, a form of Indian cheese, in most big supermarkets but for this recipe it needs to be homemade in order to achieve a lovely crumbly consistency. Serve with freshly made chapati (page 182) and a bean or lentil dish.

Serves 6

250-300g *crumbly paneer*
  (pages 257-8)
3 tbsp oil
1 tsp cumin seeds
1 medium onion, finely chopped
30g ginger, finely chopped
1 green chilli, finely chopped
½ tsp turmeric

½ tsp garam masala
½ tsp salt
50g ripe tomatoes, blended
  or 40g passata
150g fresh or frozen peas
a handful of coriander leaves,
  chopped, to garnish

Heat the oil in a karahi or sauté pan on a medium heat and add the cumin seeds, allowing them to sizzle for a few seconds. Add the onions and fry for 2 minutes. Lower the heat and add the ginger, chillies, turmeric, garam masala and salt. Stir for 2 minutes, adding a splash of water if the ingredients are sticking to the pan. Add the tomatoes, and stir for a minute.

Add the peas and cook for 2-3 minutes or until just done. Just before serving, stir in the paneer and warm through. Garnish with the chopped coriander.

GAJAR ALOO MATAR
Carrots, potatoes and peas

In the summer garden of my childhood, we grew plentiful fenugreek, coriander, potatoes, carrots and peas. These fresh vegetables would often make their way to our plates in the form of this dish. The peas were my favourite part and my mother would ask my brother and me to shell them while she prepared the rest of the dinner. They were tender, sweet and delicious, and almost half of them would always end up in our tummies rather than in the pan. Fenugreek is a green herb that looks a little bit like clover or watercress. You can find it in Asian grocery shops and some Western supermarkets. Discard any leaves that are faded and yellow and don't use the thicker stems as they will be bitter. Use this herb in moderation as it is very strongly flavoured. Serve with a lentil or bean dish and chapati (page 182).

Serves 6

3 tbsp oil
1 tbsp cumin seeds
1 medium onion, finely chopped
30g ginger, finely chopped
2 cloves garlic, finely chopped
2 green chillies, finely chopped
1 tsp turmeric
1 tsp salt

50g fenugreek leaves, finely chopped
350g ripe tomatoes, blended or 250g passata
400g carrots, cut into 1cm cubes
400g all-purpose potatoes, peeled and cut into 1cm cubes
300g fresh or frozen peas
1 tbsp garam masala

Heat the oil in a large karahi or sauté pan on a medium heat and add the cumin seeds, allowing them to sizzle for a few seconds. Add the onions and fry for 5 minutes until soft. Lower the heat and add the ginger, garlic, chillies, turmeric and salt, stirring frequently for 4-5 minutes. If the spices begin to stick to the bottom of the pan, just add a splash of water. Add the fenugreek and stir for a minute. Then add the tomatoes and, stirring occasionally, cook on a low heat for 5 minutes or until you have a thick but fairly moist sauce.

Add the carrots and potatoes, coating them with the sauce. Cover the pan and, stirring occasionally, cook over a low heat for 15-20 minutes or until the vegetables are soft, adding the peas a few minutes before the end of the cooking time. Sprinkle the garam masala over and give one more gentle stir before serving.

STUFFED OKRA

Okra, like aubergine, is definitely a taste I acquired as a teenager. Maybe if I'd been born in India, I would have got used to these exotic flavours earlier, but I think I've made up for it since! This recipe has become a great favourite with our friends. A little patience is required to fill the okra but it can be prepared beforehand and then fried a few minutes before serving. Delicious with just about everything.

Serves 6

600g okra, stalks trimmed, slit lengthways to make a little pocket
1 tbsp mango powder
1 tbsp garam masala
1 tbsp ground cumin

1 tbsp ground coriander
1 tbsp ground black pepper
½ tsp chilli powder
1½ tsp turmeric
1 tsp salt
4-5 tbsp oil

Mix all the spices together in a bowl and then, using a small spoon, fill the okra evenly with the spice mix.

Cook the okra in two batches. Heat half the oil in a large karahi or frying pan on a medium heat. Carefully lower in the okra and fry for 4-5 minutes until they are soft and slightly charred. Don't worry if some of the filling falls out, as this will add a touch of spice to the outside of the okra. Remove from the pan and set aside.

Add the remainder of the oil and cook the second batch of okra in the same way. If you want, return the first batch of okra to the pan and gently warm through.

RUNNER BEANS WITH POTATOES

One of the things I look forward to most about the summer is being able to grow and eat my own vegetables. Runner beans seem to do particularly well in this country, and I love the freshness you get from cooking them as soon as they have been picked. If you have an abundance of beans, then feel free to replace some (or all) of the potatoes with them. It's best to use beans that are fresh and tender – no one wants to chew on tough, woody ones.

Serves 6

3 tbsp oil
2 tsp cumin seeds
1 small onion, finely chopped
15g ginger, finely chopped
2 cloves garlic, finely chopped
1 green chilli, finely chopped
½ tsp turmeric
1 tsp garam masala

1 tsp salt
100g ripe tomatoes, blended
  or 80g passata
200g all-purpose potatoes, peeled
  and cut into 1.5cm cubes
450g runner beans, stalks
  trimmed, strings removed and
  cut diagonally into 3cm pieces

Heat the oil in a large karahi or sauté pan on a medium heat and add the cumin seeds, allowing them to sizzle for a few seconds. Add the onions and fry on a medium heat for 3-4 minutes. Lower the heat, add the ginger, garlic, chilli, turmeric, garam masala and salt. Stir for 3-4 minutes, adding a splash of water if the spices begin to stick.

Add the tomatoes and potatoes and give it all a stir. Cook for 5-6 minutes. Lower the heat and add the runner beans, stir gently and then cover and cook for 8-10 minutes until just done.

ALOOA DI SUBJI
Spicy potatoes

Among the ingredients you'll always find in an Indian home is the humble potato. As a youngster, I often had to dig them up and clean them. This tiresome task of my childhood has now become part of the simple pleasure of growing my own. As you can imagine, my mum was very creative with her potato dishes. With the citrusy flavour of the mango and the homely warmth of the garam masala, the potato is transformed into this deliciously appealing dish in just a few easy steps. Cut the potatoes to the same size so they cook both evenly and quickly. For something different with brunch, serve with Indian omelette (page 134) and lemon and ginger pickle (page 210).

Serves 6

3 tbsp oil
1 tbsp cumin seeds
30g ginger, finely chopped
3 cloves garlic, finely chopped
2 green chillies, finely chopped
1½ tsp mango powder
½ tsp turmeric

¾ tsp salt
400g ripe tomatoes, blended
  or 300g passata
1.2kg all-purpose potatoes, peeled
  and cut into 2cm cubes
1 tbsp garam masala

Heat the oil in a large karahi or wide pan on a medium heat and add the cumin seeds, allowing them to sizzle for a few seconds. Turn the heat to low and then add the ginger, garlic, chillies, mango powder, turmeric and salt. Cook for 2-3 minutes, stirring constantly to prevent the spices from sticking to the pan.

Now add the tomato and potatoes. Stir so that the potatoes are coated with the tomatoes. Cover and cook for 20-30 minutes, giving the pan a little jiggle every now and then. Sprinkle the garam masala over, give it one more gentle stir, and serve.

SAMBHARA
Gujarati-style carrots and cabbage

Fresh, zappy and colourful, this Gujarati dish is one that my friends often ask me to make for a 'bring-a-dish-evening'. The recipe is interesting because it contains some of the ingredients (asafoetida and neem leaves) that set Punjabi and Gujarati cuisine apart. Frying the spices in hot oil, or 'tempering' as it is known, is typical of this style of cooking. It is often done at the very start of the cooking, or at the end: in which case the spices are fried in a separate pan and then added to the cooked dish.

I only started using some of these ingredients when I met my husband, who was born in Kenya. Gujarati food is very popular there within the Indian community. As a child, however, I was familiar with the dried twigs (datun) of the neem tree, which, in India, are sometimes used in place of a toothbrush and paste. I thought it a special treat when I was allowed to chew on it to enjoy its slightly bitter taste. Neem is sold in the UK as dried curry leaves and can be found in Asian shops and supermarkets.

Remember to place the lid on the popping mustard seeds otherwise they'll be all over your kitchen floor. Serve hot or cold.

Serves 6

2 tbsp oil
1 tbsp black mustard seeds
1 tbsp cumin seeds
2 dried red chillies
10 curry (neem) leaves,
  fresh or dried
1 cinnamon stick, about 5cm
1 tsp asafoetida
1 tsp turmeric
1 tbsp sesame seeds

300g carrots, cut into
  thick 'matchsticks'
1 white cabbage (about 500g),
  quartered, then thinly sliced
  into 4cm lengths
3 green chillies, cut in
  half lengthways
1 tsp salt
1 tbsp caster sugar
juice of 2 lemons

Heat the oil in a large karahi or saucepan on a medium heat until the oil is smoking ever so slightly. Add the mustard seeds, cover with a lid until they start popping and then add the cumin seeds, red chillies, neem leaves and cinnamon stick, allowing them to sizzle for just a few seconds. Add the asafoetida and stir continuously for 30 seconds or so. Add the turmeric and sesame seeds, followed by the carrot, cabbage and green chillies. Stir to coat the vegetables with the spices. Add the salt, sugar and lemon juice.

Lower the heat, cover and cook for 8-10 minutes, stirring once or twice until the vegetables are soft but still retain a little bit of crunch.

BHARTHA
Smoky aubergine with onion and spices

Roasting aubergines over an open flame gives them a slightly smoky flavour, which will be enhanced by adding spices – although you want to avoid overpowering the dish. If you've got time, you can barbecue the aubergines for a result that will keep even the meat-eaters happy. Although the skin will be charred, even blackened, the flesh will be soft. If you like, garnish the finished bharta with crispy fried onions and chopped green chillies. Serve with a dhal, hot naan (page 186) or chapati (page 182), hot or cold on toast, or as a dip with a squeeze of lemon. If it doesn't disappear all at once, it will keep in the fridge for a couple of days.

If you're preparing the aubergines in your oven, remember to pierce them as you don't want them exploding. *Photo page 163.*

Serves 6-8 depending on how you're serving it

For the aubergine
1kg large aubergines
4 tbsp oil
1 medium onion, roughly chopped
30g ginger, finely chopped
3 cloves garlic, finely chopped
1 green chilli, finely chopped
½ tsp turmeric
½ tsp garam masala
¾ tsp salt
200g ripe tomatoes, finely chopped

For the garnish
2 tbsp oil
½ small onion, finely sliced
1 green chilli, thinly sliced on the diagonal

Prepare the aubergines

Put the aubergines on a wire rack over a low flame and cook until black and charred. Using tongs, turn the aubergines frequently so that they cook evenly. This takes about 15-20 minutes. Alternatively, if cooking in the oven, pierce the aubergines with a fork and place on a baking sheet. Bake for an hour at 200°C/400°F/Gas Mark 6 – the aubergines should be completely soft.

When cool enough to handle, cut in half, scoop out the flesh with a spoon and lightly fork through. (Discard the skins.)

Prepare the rest of the dish

Heat the oil in a medium-sized karahi or saucepan on a medium heat. Add the onions and fry for about 2-3 minutes until soft. Add the ginger, garlic, green chilli, turmeric, garam masala and salt. Turn down the heat and fry the spices for 2-3 minutes. Stir in the tomatoes, and cook for 5-6 minutes. Add the aubergines and cook for about 4-6 minutes until the moisture is almost absorbed.

Garnish

Heat the oil in a small karahi or frying pan on a medium heat, add the onions and fry for about 10-15 minutes, stirring so that they do not stick to the pan. When done, they should be soft in the middle and dark golden brown on the outside (but not burnt).

Remove from the heat with a slotted spoon and spread out on kitchen paper. Take some more kitchen paper and press down on the onions to remove any excess oil. As they cool, they will become crispy. Sprinkle them, with the green chilli, over the bhartha.

LONG R A V A

RAM TORI
Courgettes with tomatoes and lemon

In the summer months, I often end up with a glut of home-grown vegetables. It always seems to be courgettes and runner beans. The same goes for my vegetable-growing friends. How many times have I come away with a bagful of vegetables, knowing that I have more of the same at home? Anyway, for a different way to enjoy courgettes, try this super-quick recipe. The sprinkling of lemon at the end brings out the fresh summer flavours. Serve hot with lentils, or cold as a side salad for barbecues. Courgettes cook quickly, so watch them closely – transfer them to a serving dish as soon as they're done.

Serves 6

2 tbsp oil
1 tbsp cumin seeds
1 green chilli, finely chopped
¼ tsp turmeric
½ tsp sea salt flakes

50g ripe tomatoes, finely chopped
700g courgettes, cut into
    thick 'matchsticks'
a squeeze of lemon juice

Heat the oil in a large karahi or sauté pan on a medium heat and add the cumin seeds, allowing them to sizzle for a few seconds. Lower the heat and add the green chilli, turmeric and salt. Fry for a minute or two. Stir in the tomatoes. Add the courgette slices, and cook on a medium heat for 4-5 minutes or until just beginning to soften. Sprinkle the lemon juice over and serve.

NIRAJ'S CHIPS-NU-SHAAK

Gujarati-style potatoes

To paraphrase Oscar Wilde, I can resist everything except Gujarati-style potatoes – I absolutely love them! The combination of spices seems to make the potatoes explode with flavour. I had never cooked them this way before, so when my friend Niraj gave me this recipe, I rushed into the kitchen to try it. She also suggested I use a heat diffuser and now I wouldn't make this dish without one. This is a metal disc used to spread the heat more evenly across the bottom of a pan to prevent burning or sticking. They are very cheap and can normally be found in most Asian supermarkets.

Line up your spices beforehand in the order given below. They cook very quickly and within seconds of each other and you don't want to end up burning them. Note that you can either slice the potatoes for crispiness, or cube them for a softer end result. Neither will disappoint.

Serves 6-8

3 tbsp oil
1 tbsp cumin seeds
2 dried red chillies
10 curry leaves (neem), fresh or dried
1 tsp asafoetida

1.2kg potatoes – either new potatoes, sliced (about the thickness of a £1 coin), or any other waxy potato, peeled and cut into 1.5cm cubes
1 green chilli, sliced lengthways
¾ tsp salt
1 tsp ground black pepper

Heat the oil in a large karahi or wide-bottomed saucepan on a medium heat and add the cumin seeds, followed by the red chillies, neem leaves and then the asafoetida. Allow them to sizzle for 20-30 seconds in which time their colours should deepen.

Add the potatoes, sliced green chilli, salt and pepper. Give a good stir so the potatoes are completely flecked with the spices. This is where to place the heat diffuser on the stovetop, if you're using one. Cover the pan and allow the potatoes to cook in their own steam for 20-25 minutes, giving the pan an occasional gentle stir.

TANGY OKRA WITH ONION

As with the other okra recipes, it's vital to use the freshest you can find. Here, the distinct flavour is created by combining the earthy-tasting okra with the sweetness of the onion, the peppery warmth of the mustard seeds and the fruity tartness of the mango. Your taste buds then receive a final smack from the sea salt. This is quite a strong-flavoured dish and maybe one for the more adventurous palates. That said, it's these flavours that also make it an ideal side dish for urid dhal (page 110) or for one of the richer meat curries.

Serves 6

10 tbsp oil
1 tbsp black mustard seeds
2 medium onions,
   not too thinly sliced
1 tbsp ground cumin
1 tsp mango powder

½ tsp chilli flakes
30g ginger, finely chopped
3 cloves garlic, finely chopped
600g okra, stalks trimmed,
   cut in half lengthways
1 tsp sea salt flakes

Heat 4 tbsp of the oil in a large karahi or frying pan on a medium heat and add the mustard seeds, allowing them to pop for a few seconds. Add the onions and fry for 9-10 minutes until soft and dark golden. Add the cumin, mango powder and chilli, and stir for 2 minutes. Add the ginger and garlic and a few splashes of water if the mixture starts sticking to the pan. Cook for 3-4 minutes. Set aside.

Now cook the okra in two batches. To do this, heat a separate karahi or frying pan until it's really hot and then add 3 tbsp of oil – it will be smoking slightly. Stir-fry the okra until cooked; it will be browned in places but still retain a bit of crunch. Remove from the pan and set aside.

Add the remainder of the oil for the second batch, get it hot and smoking again, and stir-fry the okra in the same way. Add the first batch of okra back into the pan, sprinkle the salt over and give it a quick stir. Add the onion mixture, and heat for 20-30 seconds, stirring gently. Serve hot or cold.

ROASTED CAULIFLOWER

This beautiful, golden cauliflower takes just 10 minutes to prepare with a short spell in the oven. The lemon juice really makes this dish 'sing' by giving a lift to the slightly charred flavours of the spices and cauliflower. The cauliflower should have a bit of bite so, to avoid overcooking, don't cut the florets too small. This dish is great with any of the lentil, bean or meat curry recipes, as a salad, or even to accompany a Western-style Sunday roast. In the summer, I finish it off on the barbecue for about 5 minutes to bring out those smoky flavours that suit cauliflower so well.

Serves 6

5 tbsp oil
¼ tsp chilli flakes (optional)
1 tbsp garam masala
½ tsp turmeric

1 large cauliflower, cut into medium-sized florets
a sprinkling of sea salt flakes
juice of 1 lemon

Preheat the oven to 180°C/350°F/Gas Mark 4.

Heat the oil in a large karahi or deep frying pan on a medium heat and add the chilli flakes, garam masala, and turmeric, and fry for 1 minute or so. Turn off the heat.

Add the cauliflower to the pan and sprinkle over the salt. Stir so that the florets are completely coated with the spices, then spread evenly into a shallow ovenproof dish. Roast for 20-25 minutes. Sprinkle the lemon juice over and serve.

STUFFED AUBERGINES

If you've been reading this book from cover to cover, you might have noticed that I have a weakness for aubergines. There is a huge variety to choose from: if you go to an Asian market, the aubergines might well outdo the potatoes for choice. You will see vegetables that are small or large, round and plump, thin and long, pear-shaped or apple-shaped, and in colours of white, cream, green, orange, yellow or purple, multi-coloured – even striped!

Don't attempt to eat aubergine raw, as it will be terribly bitter. Its true flavours are revealed when it is cooked. Depending on which variety you pick, and how you prepare it, the flavour and texture will vary from mild and delicate to rich and creamy. It can be roasted, grilled, fried, braised with other vegetables, mashed for a dip or, as my aunts would do, prepared as a pickle. Here, the sweetness of the tomato sauce complements the delicate flavour of the aubergines perfectly. Make sure you use the smaller, Indian variety. Cook the sauce until it's thick, so it stays in the aubergine.

Serves 6

3 tbsp oil
1 tbsp cumin seeds
1 large onion, finely chopped
30g ginger, finely chopped
4 cloves garlic, finely chopped
2 green chillies, finely chopped
1 tsp turmeric

1 tsp garam masala
1½ tsp salt
250g ripe tomatoes, blended
  or 200g passata
12 small plump aubergines
a little oil, to brush onto the
  baking dish

Heat the oil in a karahi or saucepan on a medium heat and add the cumin seeds, allowing them to sizzle for a few seconds. Add the onions and fry for 7-8 minutes until deep brown. Add the ginger, garlic and chillies, and fry for 2 minutes, stirring constantly. Then add the turmeric, garam masala and salt and fry for a further 2 minutes, continuing to stir. Add the tomatoes and cook for 8-10 minutes, or until you have a very thick sauce, stirring occasionally.

Preheat the oven to 180°C/350°F/Gas Mark 4.

Using a small sharp knife, cut the tops off the aubergines and then cut two slits (crossways) from there, three quarters of the way down each one. Prise out the seeds by turning and twisting the knife. Divide the tomato sauce into twelve equal portions and spoon into the aubergines, filling the aubergines as deeply as possible.

Lightly oil a shallow baking dish. Lay the aubergines on their sides making sure that they are not touching each other. Bake for 40-50 minutes, covering with parchment paper (or foil) halfway through. When done, the aubergines should be soft and slightly charred.

TINDORI
!7aa

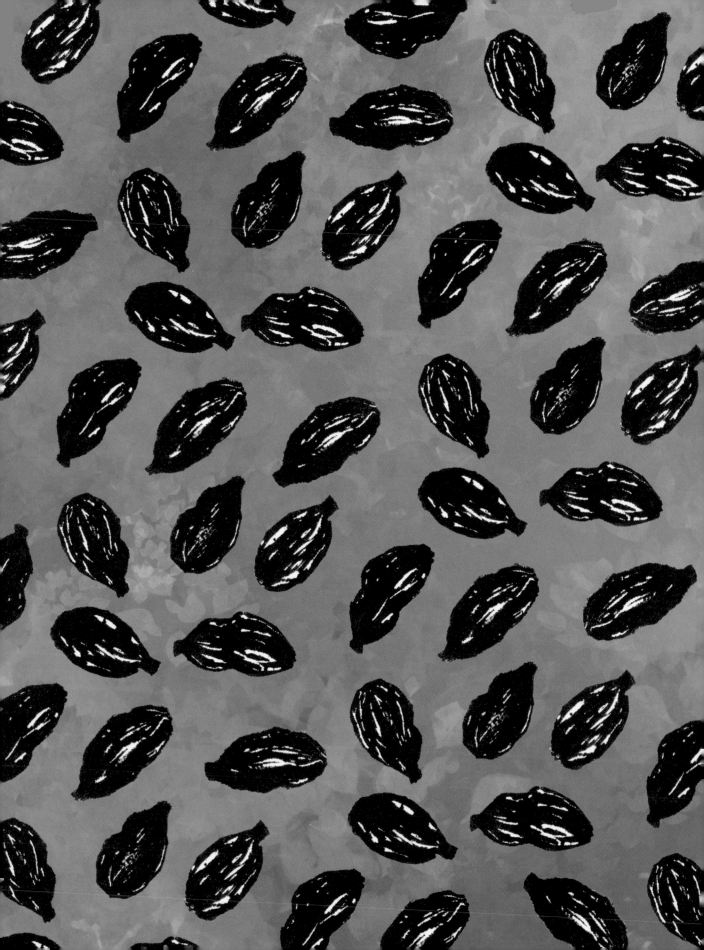

RICE AND BREADS

Tender fluffy rice and wholesome hot breads

Rice and bread are the staple foods in India. For Punjabis, such as my parents, no meal would be complete without chapati. Whereas for Gujaratis, rice is the key to satisfaction, as I learnt from one of my husband's colleagues, a proud Gujarati himself. That was when I really became aware that our palates – all of them accustomed to the flavours of India – could nevertheless differ over the most basic of things.

Unlike Western-style bread, Indian flatbreads such as chapati, poori and paratha are used in place of cutlery. With your thumb and first two fingers, break off a little bit of the flat bread and use it to pick up your food, or shape it into a triangle and use it like a scoop. Do this with confidence – don't be embarrassed – and before long you will have mastered the art of eating by hand.

Indian rice is synonymous with basmati: long-grained, with a fragrant and nutty flavour. When cooked, the grains remain separate, light and fluffy. Don't just grab any rice from your cupboard. Basmati is the one that will give the final flourish of flavour to your food.

If you haven't got a tawa (page 182), a pan specially designed for cooking flatbreads, use a heavy-based frying pan. For the rice, use a heavy-based saucepan.

Follow these recipes and have fun rolling out the breads and producing the finest cooked rice.

ROTI
Chapati (unleavened flatbread)

Roti, or chapati as it known here, is a staple in the Punjabi home, just like potatoes for the British, or pasta for the Italians. Made from Indian durum wheat flour, it not only provides nourishment but also serves as an eating utensil.

To give you some idea of how many rotis were consumed at home, my mum kept a big steel drum in the understairs cupboard, which stored the flour or atta as we familiarly called it. It was bought in 20kg bags, not the measly 1.5kg bags that I buy!

The rotis are cooked on a tawa, a flat cast-iron pan that gives an even heat across its surface and is ideal for flipping the roti. You can buy one from most Indian stores. Alternatively, use a heavy-based frying pan. Be careful when turning the roti – it's best to use tongs or a spatula until you're more experienced, when you will be able to use your hands. My mum can make one roti a minute, although I must admit it takes me double the time. Roti goes well with almost any recipe apart from barbecued dishes, where naan (page 186) is better.

At the Gurdwara, the priest will often ask for volunteers from the congregation to help in the kitchen. As a child, I would tag along with my mother or aunts and make my small contribution to preparing lunch for the worshippers. My rotis were always rolled out into all shapes and sizes, as if they were different countries of the world – but how else would I have learnt? Still, if at first you produce a map of the world, you will only get better with practice.

See the introduction to this section (page 181) for instructions on how to eat roti.
Photo page 184.

Serves 5-6   350g chapati flour (atta),
                       plus a little extra for dusting
                    200-300ml water
                    a little butter, to spread over
                       the cooked roti (optional)

Mix the flour and water together in a large bowl. Knead until the dough is soft and pliable. Add more water if necessary. The resulting dough should peel away from the sides of the bowl. Alternatively, use a food processor and mix until the dough is formed into a ball. Sprinkle a few drops of water over, cover, and leave to rest for 30 minutes.

Knead again for a minute or so. Break off pieces of dough so that you have approximately 12 equal portions and keep covered with a damp tea towel so they don't dry out.

Heat the tawa on a medium heat until hot.

Lightly dust your work surface with flour and also pat a little onto the palm of your hands to prevent the dough from sticking. Shape a portion into a ball and lightly flatten it as much as you can with your hands, to make it easier to roll out. Sprinkle both sides with flour. Then, using a rolling pin, roll out into a circle with a diameter of about 12cm. Take the flattened dough and slap it from hand to hand to stretch it out a little.

Carefully put it onto the tawa and leave for 20-30 seconds or until little bubbles form on top. Turn it over for about 20 seconds and very lightly press down on it with a spatula so the roti cooks evenly. Using tongs, place the first side you cooked down onto the direct flame until the roti puffs up. Take care when doing this. If you don't have a gas cooker, don't worry; just turn the chapati over on the tawa again for 15-20 seconds to finish it off.

Spread the roti with butter and serve immediately or keep them covered in a tea towel until ready to eat. Repeat this process for the remainder of the dough.

NAAN
(leavened flatbread)

This bread is one of the most well-known and best-loved of all Indian foods. I love the colour, with its warm tones, I love its taste, especially when slightly charred, and I love that satisfaction of tearing off great big fluffy chunks to scoop up your food or to wipe your plate clean.

Perfecting the recipe for naan was quite difficult. Over the years, I've experimented with making naan in various ways and with different ingredients to get that authentic taste and this is the one that works best for me.

There are a few things to take note of when making naan bread. When you're mixing the ingredients, don't be tempted to add more water because as soon as you start to knead the dough it will begin to soften. The temperature of your cooking pan should be hot, but not so hot as to burn the naan. Lastly, the flame should be strong enough to allow the naans to puff up. In any case, you'll soon get the knack after preparing one or two.

In the same way as for chapatis, it's much better to use a tawa, a flat cast-iron pan that gives an even heat across its surface and is ideal for flipping the naans. You can buy one from most Indian stores. Alternatively, use a heavy-based frying pan.

See the introduction to this section (page 181) for instructions on how to eat naan.
Photos pages 188-9.

Serves 4-6

1 tsp easy-blend yeast
190ml warm water
500g plain flour, plus a
   little extra for dusting
1¼ tsp salt
1¼ tsp caster sugar

1 tbsp extra virgin olive oil
150g natural yogurt
a handful of coriander leaves,
   roughly chopped (optional)
a knob of butter, to serve
   (optional)

Add the yeast to the water in a small bowl. Whisk with a fork and set aside. Sift the flour into a large bowl. Make a well in the middle and then add the salt, sugar, oil and yogurt. Pour in the yeast water, a little at a time. Draw the mixture together with a large spoon. It will look a bit dry and messy at this stage.

Place the mixture on a work surface and knead the dough for about 5-7 minutes or until it is soft, stretchy and firm. The stickiness will disappear as you knead, so don't be tempted to add more flour. Shape into a ball, place in a clean bowl, cover with a damp tea towel and leave in a warm place (such as an airing cupboard) for about 90 minutes or so. It should double in size.

Add the chopped coriander and knead the dough again gently for 1-2 minutes or until all the air has been knocked out. Divide into 12 portions and keep covered with a damp tea towel so they don't dry out.

Heat the tawa or frying pan on a medium heat until it is hot.

Very lightly dust your work surface with flour and also pat a little onto the palm of your hands to prevent the dough from sticking. Shape a portion into a ball and lightly flatten it as much as you can with your hands, to make it easier to roll out. Sprinkle both sides with flour. Then, using a rolling pin, roll out into a circle with a diameter of 12cm. Take the rolled dough and slap it from hand to hand to stretch it out a little.

Carefully put it onto the tawa and leave for 20-30 seconds or until little bubbles form on top. Then turn it over for about 20 seconds and very lightly press down on it with a spatula so the naan cooks evenly. Using tongs, place the first side you cooked down onto the direct flame until the naan puffs up. Take care when doing this. If you don't have a gas cooker, don't worry; just turn the naan over on the tawa again for 15-20 seconds to finish it off.

Spread the hot naan with butter and serve immediately, or keep it covered with a tea towel until ready to eat. Repeat this process for the remainder of the dough.

POORI
Deep-fried bread

These golden fluffy pooris are usually served for festive occasions, such as Diwali, although they always make a satisfying dish for a special breakfast or brunch. It's best to fry the pooris just before serving so they don't lose their puffiness and go flat. They go especially well with chickpeas (page 104), aubergines with potatoes (page 146), or minced lamb (page 72) with tomato and onion salad (page 212) on the side.

This dish is traditionally eaten by breaking off a piece of the poori with your hands, scooping up a small mouthful of food and savouring it for a few seconds before having a bite of the tomato and onion salad for a mouth-watering taste sensation.

See the introduction to this section (page 181) for instructions on how to eat poori.

Serves 5-7

300g chapati flour (atta),
   plus a little extra for your hands
200-250ml water

1 tbsp oil, plus a little extra to
   sprinkle over the dough balls
oil, for deep-frying

Mix the flour, water and oil together in a large bowl. Knead until the dough is soft and pliable. Add more water if necessary. The resulting dough should peel away from the sides of the bowl. Alternatively, use a food processor and mix until the dough is formed into a ball. Place a damp tea towel (or cling film) over the bowl and leave to rest for 30 minutes.

Knead again for 2 minutes. Pat a little flour onto the palm of your hands to prevent the dough from sticking. Break off pieces of dough so that you have approximately 15 equal portions. Shape each portion into a ball and place on a large plate. Sprinkle a little oil over the dough balls, place in a bowl and lightly swirl them around with your hand so that they are evenly coated. This will prevent them from sticking to each other and they will be easier to roll out. Working with one ball at a time, flatten it as much as you can with your hands. Then, using a rolling pin, roll out into a circle with a diameter of about 10cm.

Heat the oil in a large karahi or deep pan on a medium heat until it is hot.

Slide each poori carefully into the hot oil. As soon as it rises to the surface, push it back down with the back of a slotted spoon. The poori should puff up. Fry for 10-15 seconds, then turn over and fry for another 10-15 seconds, gently pressing down with the spoon. The poori should be a lovely golden colour. Lift out with the spoon and drain on kitchen paper before serving. Repeat this process for the remainder of the dough. Serve immediately.

ALOOA DI PARATHE

Potato – stuffed chapatis

Alooa di parathe are my absolute favourite. On a Sunday morning, if my mother announced she was making them for breakfast, any need to have a lie-in was quickly forgotten. These parathe are really two chapatis joined together with the surprise of the warm spicy mashed potato inside. To further tantalise your taste buds, serve with lemon or mango pickle (pages 210, 226) and cool refreshing yogurt (page 222). A cup of tea afterwards and your meal will be truly complete! Savour each mouthful and, if you're indulging in more than one, have a break between each paratha as they really are very filling. The potato will be steaming hot, so be patient and let the paratha cool just a touch. Makes 6 parathe.

As with the chapati recipe, it's much better to use a tawa, a flat cast-iron pan that gives an even heat across its surface and is ideal for flipping the parathe. You can buy one from most Indian stores. Alternatively, use a large, heavy-based, frying pan.

In case you're wondering why there are two spellings here, *paratha* is singular and *parathe* is plural. *Photos pages 194-5.*

Serves 3-4

For the potato stuffing
400g all-purpose potatoes,
   boiled and mashed
2 green chillies, finely chopped
1½ tbsp garam masala
1 tsp ground black pepper
¾ tsp salt
30g butter, for sautéing
   the potatoes
a knob of butter, to spread
   onto the parathe

For the chapati
350g chapati flour (atta), plus a
   little extra for dusting
200-250ml water

Prepare the potato stuffing
Mix together the potato, chillies, garam masala, black pepper and salt. Melt the butter in a frying pan on a medium heat and sauté the potato mixture for about 2 minutes. Don't let it stick to the pan otherwise the potato will crisp up. Place in a bowl to cool.

Prepare the chapati
Mix the flour and water together in a large bowl. Knead until the dough is soft and pliable. Add more water if necessary. The resulting dough should peel away from the sides of the bowl. Alternatively, use a food processor and mix until the dough is formed into a ball. Place a damp tea towel (or cling film) over the bowl and leave to rest for 30 minutes.

Knead again for a minute or so. Divide the dough into 12 equal portions and keep covered with a damp tea towel so they don't dry out while you work.

Assemble the parathe
Lightly dust your work surface with flour, and also pat a little onto your palms to prevent the dough from sticking. Prepare two portions of the dough at a time. Shape each portion into a ball and lightly flatten it as much as you can with your hands, to make it easier to roll out. Sprinkle both flat sides with flour. Then, using a rolling pin, roll out into a circle with a diameter of about 10cm.

Spread a little butter over each portion and cover one buttered chapati with a sixth of your potato filling. Lay the second chapati over the first one with the buttered side touching the potato. Press the edges together to seal. Roll gently to make a few centimetres bigger.

Heat your tawa or heavy-based frying pan on a medium heat until hot.

Put the paratha on to the tawa and leave for 30 seconds. Flip it over. Do this a few times every 20-30 seconds or so until it is cooked. It should be slightly browned with little charred, dark spots. Smear one side with butter. Repeat this process for the remainder of the dough. Best served hot.

CHAUL

Plain rice

An Indian proverb says, "Perfectly cooked rice grains are like brothers: close, but not stuck together". However, it can sometimes seem a challenge to produce rice that's 'just right'. Although I've used precise measurements in this recipe, the basic principle is roughly one part rice to one and a half parts water: this really is a reliable way to cook great rice. Be sure to use basmati to give you that truly Indian taste – any other kind of rice just won't be the same. At the end of the cooking time, even if you think the rice needs a few minutes more, it doesn't – trust me! See the Glossary (page 258) for more about basmati rice.

Serves 6

350g basmati rice, rinsed
and soaked in cold water
for 30 minutes
850ml freshly boiled water

Rinse and drain the rice thoroughly.

Put the rice into a large heavy-bottomed saucepan and add the water. On a medium heat, bring to the boil and then continue cooking on a low heat for 4-5 minutes or until the bubbles of water have almost disappeared. Then cover the pan completely and cook for another 2-3 minutes. Keep the lid firmly on, as the steam will allow the rice to cook fully.

Remove the pan from the heat and leave to stand for 5 minutes. Then lightly fluff up the rice with a fork to separate the grains and serve.

MATARA DI CHAUL
Rice with peas

When I was a child, we had roti for dinner almost every day. It was only on rare occasions, when we were having chicken, that my mother would ask us if we wanted matara di chaul. The answer was always "Yes". The fresh sweet tones of the peas are a perfect match for the savoury rice. The secret to the rice tasting good is to keep it moist, so don't uncover the pan too early once the lid is on, otherwise too much of the steam will escape. Even so, your kitchen will be filled with the fragrance of this light but intensely flavoured dish. Serve with meat and fish dishes, or with beans and lentils, but it's especially good with Biji's chicken (page 56). See the Glossary (page 258) for more about basmati rice.

For jeera (cumin) rice, follow the instructions below but omit the steps for the onion and peas.

Serves 6

350g basmati rice, rinsed
  and soaked in cold water
  for 30 minutes
50g unsalted butter
1 tbsp cumin seeds

1 large onion, sliced
300g fresh or frozen peas
1 tsp salt
800ml freshly boiled water

Rinse and drain the rice thoroughly and set aside.

Melt the butter in a large heavy-bottomed saucepan on a medium heat. Add the cumin seeds and fry for 20 seconds. Add the onion and fry for about 4-5 minutes until translucent. Then add the rice to the pan and fry on a low heat for about 2-3 minutes, stirring regularly so that it does not stick. The rice will change to a light golden colour.

Add the peas. Then, add the salt and the water and bring to the boil – do not stir. Cook on a low heat for a further 5-6 minutes, or until the bubbles of water have almost disappeared. Cover the pan completely and cook on a low heat for another 2-3 minutes.

Remove from the heat and leave to stand for 5 minutes. Then lightly fluff up the rice with a fork to separate the grains and serve.

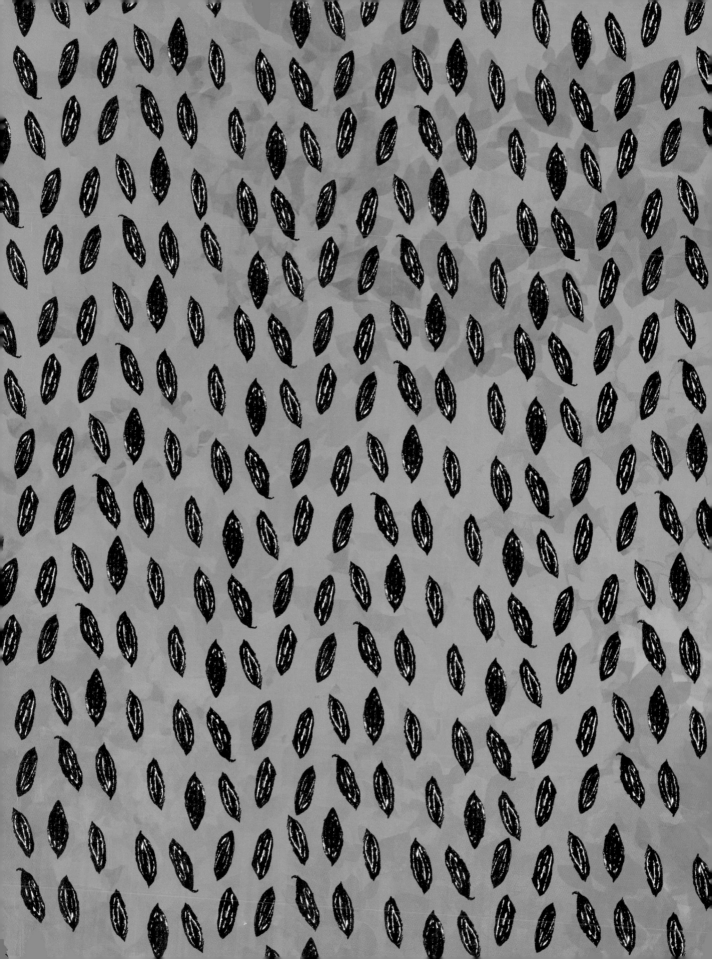

ON THE SIDE

Refreshing salads, fiery pickles, spicy chutneys and cooling yogurts

There is something almost magical about the accompaniments to an Indian meal. Even the modest dhal-roti (lentils and chapati) becomes something special when adorned with the bold, deep flavours of lemon pickle and a cooling bowl of yogurt. Add a colourful, crunchy salad and you are well on your way to having a feast.

Attractive and vibrant, these mouth-watering dishes can challenge your taste buds, even when eaten on their own – I guarantee that they will leave you craving for more. They are there to add texture, and complement and balance the flavours of your food. For example, a simple raita will add a refreshing sparkle to the lavish and aromatic flavours of a biryani, hot chilli barbecued prawns are transformed by coconut and coriander chutney, mint chutney will intensify the rich subdued flavours of lamb kebabs, while a tangy tomato and onion salad brings life to the mellow earthiness of aubergines and potatoes.

These little extras constantly change and multiply the food sensations you can create and experience. So choose your flavour palette and let these accompaniments take you there!

COCONUT AND CORIANDER CHUTNEY

The mild flavours of the shredded coconut and the smooth yogurt are combined with coriander and chillies to make a light and refreshing chutney. Serve with the fish and prawn dishes, or as an accompaniment to any of the barbecue recipes. Also great as a dip, or even as a dressing for a chunky salad.

Serves 6

250g natural yogurt
40g coriander leaves
40g unsweetened
    desiccated coconut
2 green chillies
½ tsp salt

Put all the ingredients in a food processor and whizz through for about thirty seconds, or until everything is smooth and well blended.

KACHUMBER

Tomato and cucumber salad

This light, vibrant salad with its tangy flavours contrasts perfectly with the spiciness of an Indian meal.

Serves 6

1 medium-sized cucumber,
    cut into 1cm cubes
6 medium-sized ripe tomatoes,
    cut into 1cm cubes

½ tsp sea salt flakes
a handful of coriander leaves,
    chopped fairly coarsely
juice of 1 lemon or lime

Put all the ingredients in a bowl and drizzle over the juice. Gently mix the salad together just before serving.

MANGO CHUTNEY

Peeling the mangoes is a bit fiddly but once the ingredients are in the pan, all you have to do is keep a watchful eye on the cooking time. Sweet and spicy, this chutney can be served with any of the main course dishes. You could try it with scrambled eggs, an omelette, or even in a sandwich. It will keep its fruity freshness for a few days stored in the fridge.

Makes a small jar

1.5kg firm ripe mangoes, washed, skinned, seeded and chopped roughly into chunks (you'll need about 750g mango flesh)
½ tsp cumin seeds
1 tsp coriander seeds, lightly crushed
15g fresh ginger, peeled and finely chopped

2 garlic cloves, finely chopped
¼ tsp red chilli flakes
1 tsp black peppercorns
1 cinnamon stick, about 3cm
½ tsp black mustard seeds or nigella seeds
100g caster sugar
½ tsp salt
100ml malt vinegar

Put all the ingredients into a medium-sized karahi or heavy-bottomed saucepan. Bring to the boil and then cook on a very low heat for about 35-40 minutes or until the fruit is soft and smooth. Stir occasionally, particularly towards the end of the cooking time, so that the chutney does not stick to the bottom of the pan.

NIMBOO ADRAK DA ACHAAR

Lemon and ginger pickle

This sharp citrus pickle really adds a whole new dimension to almost any Indian meal. It's best eaten one or two weeks after preparation, when the lemons are tender and the flavours have developed, although it never seems to last that long in our house. Traditionally, in India, the lemons would be left to soften in the hot rays of the sun. Here, I have gently simmered them so that they have only just lost their firmness. Because the salt both softens and preserves the lemons, it's important to give your jar a good shake so the salt is evenly distributed. Once the jar is opened, I keep it in the fridge so it stays fresh.

Makes enough
to fill a large jar
(500-750g)

1 tbsp carom seeds
4 lemons, washed
enough water to cover the lemons
200g ginger, cut into thick slivers
½ tsp chilli flakes
1½ tsp turmeric
3 tbsp salt

Heat a small pan on a really low heat until just hot and then dry roast the carom seeds until they change colour. This will only take 15-20 seconds so keep a close eye on them. Remove from the pan and put aside on a plate.

Put the lemons and water into a pan and bring to the boil. Cover with a lid and simmer for 3-4 minutes. The lemons should be slightly soft but still hold their shape. Drain, and leave until cool enough to handle.

Halve each lemon lengthways and then cut each half into three or four pieces, reserving any juice that runs out. Carefully remove the seeds. Put the lemons and their juice into a bowl. Add the ginger, carom seeds, chilli flakes, turmeric and salt. Stir gently to coat the lemons with the spices.

Spoon the mixture into a sterilised jar. Seal with the lid and leave standing for 5 days or so, giving it a good shake a couple of times a day to ensure the lemons are covered with the juice they release. Just take out as much as you need with a clean dry spoon and replace the lid. Should keep for a month or more – pickle-thieves permitting!

Lemon & ginger pickle
03/11/2016

TOMATO AND ONION SALAD

This salad is the most popular accompaniment to a real Punjabi meal. It is easy to prepare and can be eaten with your fingers. Try taking a mouthful of your main dish with a bite of the tomato or onion, then wait as the chilli, salt and lime combine to produce an explosion of flavours.

Replace the tomato and onion with fiery white radish and sweet carrots to make an equally enjoyable salad.

Serves 6

2 medium-sized ripe tomatoes,
    thickly sliced
1 medium onion,
    thickly sliced

a pinch of chilli flakes
a pinch of sea salt flakes
juice of 1 lemon or lime

Mix all the ingredients in a bowl and serve.

IMLI DI CHUTNEY

Tamarind chutney

Tamarind is a fruit that is grown widely in India and is popular in both savoury and sweet dishes. It is sold in Asian shops and nowadays even in many Western supermarkets, as compressed blocks or as a concentrate. In the block form, the outer shell of the fruit has been removed to leave the seeds and sticky pods. If you are using it like this in your cooking it is very difficult to give exact measurements, so you might need to experiment. I suggest starting with about 25g of tamarind. Pour 80ml hot water over the pods and leave for 30 minutes or so. Then press the pulp through a sieve. You will end up with a thick mushy liquid. Discard the fibrous strands left behind. This is how my mother prepares imli but it's a bit fiddly. Personally, I prefer to use concentrate – far simpler and quicker. There is a difference in taste but, in my opinion, it's not so noticeable that it really affects the final flavour of the chutney.

Getting the balance of sweet, sour, salt and chilli just right is not as easy as it might look. No one ingredient should steal the show. I normally make this by constantly tasting it as I go along. After watching me preparing it in my usual instinctive way, my friends, Gillian and Alison, wanted to write the recipe for this chutney; I didn't think they would master the process but they proved me wrong! Their persistence in measuring every minuscule quantity of the ingredients means we now have the perfect recipe and it's actually easy-peasy.

Tart tamarind makes a mouth-watering accompaniment to samosas (page 20), potato fritters (page 24) and sheekh kebabs (page 34). It can be used to liven up roasted vegetables like sweet potatoes, roasted carrots and aubergines, as a salad dressing, or even as a refreshing drink when it has been diluted with water. For the more adventurous, try it drizzled lightly over fruit. (See the recipe on page 234 for ideas about which fruit to use.)

Be sure to use thick tamarind concentrate, not the ready-flavoured sauce that is sold in some supermarkets.

Makes 60ml

20ml cold water
1 tbsp tamarind concentrate
½ tsp ground black pepper

½ tsp salt or 1 tsp sea salt flakes
¼ tsp chilli flakes
1 tbsp caster sugar

Mix all the ingredients together thoroughly in a bowl using a fork or a small whisk. It will keep in a jar in the fridge for at least a week.

PODINI DI CHUTNEY
Mint chutney

One of the joys of writing this book has been to stir up those long lost memories of childhood. How often I would watch my mother as she sat on the back doorstep with the pestle and mortar in front of her for hours on end, sometimes grinding nuts, sometimes making garam masala and sometimes, for this chutney, pressing and crushing, squashing and beating.

Now, of course, we have the food processor. Either way, you will have lip-smacking chutney. The pomegranate adds a tangy flavour. Fire up your barbecue to enjoy this chutney with sheekh kebabs (page 34) or lamb chops (page 76), or get busy in the kitchen to prepare Gujarati-style savoury cakes (page 46) or potato fritters (page 24).

Serves 6

1 tbsp tamarind concentrate
75-100ml water
1 tsp ground black pepper
1 tsp pomegranate powder or
   2 tbsp fresh pomegranate
   (optional)

1 tsp salt
1½ tsp sugar
60g fresh mint leaves
2 green chillies
½ medium onion

Blend the tamarind and water in a food processor. Add the remaining ingredients and process until smooth or, if you prefer, just slightly coarse.

LASSI

Zingy and refreshing, luscious and creamy – this yogurt drink is great on a hot summer's day.

Serves 4

500g *yogurt* (page 222)
1 tsp *chaat masala* (page 254)
200ml cold water

Mix all the ingredients in a jug or blender and whisk until frothy. Pour over ice cubes in tall glasses and enjoy.

CARROT AND GREEN CHILLI SALAD

This is definitely a chilli lover's recipe. Depending on how spicy you like things, it can even be enjoyed as a snack. Otherwise, try serving it with some of the richer dishes in this book. You could dice it up into fried rice or use it to pep up other salads. Measure out the spices beforehand, as you need to add them quickly to the hot oil, otherwise they will burn and your dish will taste bitter. Be sure to stick to the order in which they are listed below, as they require different cooking times.

Every December, I have a big dinner party when the boys do all the cooking and serving. A year never goes by without at least one of my friends mistaking the chillies in this dish for some mild, green vegetable. Out come the yogurt, milk, water and sugar or whatever helps to numb the pain. Even wine has been tried – it doesn't work!

Serves 8-10
(or one chilli fanatic!)

4 tbsp oil
1 tbsp black mustard seeds
1 tsp cumin seeds
10 curry (neem) leaves,
    fresh or dried
1 cinnamon stick, about 5cm
2 tsp asafoetida
2 tsp sesame seeds

1½ tsp turmeric powder
1 tsp sea salt flakes
250g carrots, cut into thick
    'matchsticks' about 5cm long
20 long green chillies, stalks
    removed, 10 left whole and
    10 cut in half lengthways
juice of 2 lemons

Heat the oil in a large karahi or frying pan on a medium heat until the oil is smoking ever so slightly. Add the mustard seeds, cover with a lid until they start popping and then add the cumin seeds, neem leaves and cinnamon stick, allowing them to sizzle for a few seconds. Add the asafoetida, and stir continuously for 30 seconds or so in which time the colours should deepen. Now add the sesame seeds, turmeric and salt. Stir for a minute or until the spices have all changed colour.

Add the carrots and stir for 1-2 minutes, making sure that the vegetables are completely covered with the spices. The carrots should be soft but retain a little crunchiness. Add the chillies, stir for about 15 seconds, then sprinkle the lemon juice over. Cool and put in a jar or small serving dish. The salad will keep for 2-3 days in the fridge.

DAHI
Homemade yogurt

I grew up on homemade yogurt and now I always have a supply of it in the fridge. Typically, yogurt is served as part of the main course but I love it so much that I always leave it for last. That said, I would certainly reach for it sooner if anything proves to be a bit too hot, as in chilli-hot.

To turn milk into yogurt, you need the 'active' culture (or bacteria) that is found in 'live' yogurt. You can buy this from most supermarkets. Using whole milk makes for a thicker, creamier yogurt but semi-skimmed works, too. You will need a container in which to ferment the milk and somewhere to keep it warm, like an airing cupboard. My mother has used the same pot for 40 years and wraps it in an old woollen jumper, so you could even use a tea cosy. It then takes between 4-10 hours to turn into yogurt. The longer you leave it, the more it sets and the more tart it becomes. Remember to keep a tablespoon of the yogurt you make, ready to prepare your next batch.

With this recipe, you can choose whether to make plain natural yogurt or, with a few more easy steps, the Greek-style version.

Makes 500g of natural yogurt or 250g of Greek yogurt

1 litre whole milk
1 tbsp 'live' natural yogurt

Bring the milk to the boil and then pour into a heatproof container. Cool until it is 'warm' rather than 'hot' – you should be able to touch it comfortably. Stir in the tablespoon of 'live' yogurt, including any skin that has formed on top of the milk. Cover with a lid, wrap it up in something warm (a blanket, a coat, a tea cosy...) and place somewhere warm (see above). Let it ferment for 4-10 hours.

Check to see if it is set by gently tilting the container. If it moves in one mass, you'll know it's ready. Put in the fridge to chill and to set a bit more.

If you want the consistency of Greek yogurt, place a muslin-lined sieve over a bowl. Pour in the yogurt and leave in the fridge for a couple of hours to let the whey trickle through into the bowl. The longer you leave it, the thicker it will be. If you find that it has thickened too much, thin it down by stirring some of the whey back into the yogurt.

RAITA

Yogurt with cucumber

My mother made yogurt every day and it was always part of our evening meal. She would prepare it at night and by the following morning the yogurt would be set. For special occasions we would have this raita. The yogurt, mint, and the lemony flavour of coriander all combine to provide a zappy contrast to other Indian dishes. The cucumber is salted to remove the moisture and prevent the dish becoming watery. I always include a chilli for an extra kick.

Serves 6

½ cucumber, skin on
   and finely chopped
½ tsp salt
400g *yogurt* (page 222)
a handful of mint leaves, chopped

a handful of coriander leaves,
   roughly chopped
1 green chilli, chopped (optional)
a little freshly ground black pepper

Put the cucumber into a large sieve placed over a bowl. Sprinkle the salt over the cucumber and give it a gentle stir. Set aside for 30 minutes. Put the cucumber between two sheets of kitchen paper and press firmly to squeeze out the water.

Put the yogurt into a bowl. Just before serving, add the cucumber to the yogurt. Gently stir in the remainder of the ingredients.

AMB DA ACHAAR

Mango pickle

To double-check this recipe, my Aunt Surinder made a quick phone call to my cousin in India. Her name, coincidentally, is also Balwinder, and her contribution to this book was to suggest adding a little oil to help preserve the mangoes. Apart from that, it seemed I had passed the test!

You can eat this pickle immediately after it's made but, to enjoy it to its full, you really should leave it for a day or two so that the mangoes absorb the flavours of the spices in which they are marinated. As with the lemon pickle, always use a clean dry spoon to scoop the pickle from the jar – this will help it retain its freshness.

See the Glossary (page 258) for more about raw green mangoes.

Makes enough
to fill a large jar

500g raw green mangoes,
  skin on, sliced or cut into
  even-sized chunks
1 tsp fennel seeds
1 tsp coriander seeds, crushed

½ tsp nigella seeds
½ tsp chilli flakes
1 tsp turmeric
1½ tsp salt
3 tbsp oil

Put the mangoes in a bowl and add all the dry spices. Leave to stand in the sun for 2-3 days to release the moisture from the mangoes and spices.

Put the mango mix in a sterilised jar. Heat the oil until it is just slightly smoking. Allow to cool and then pour over the mangoes. Close the lid tightly. Leave to stand for a few days and shake the jar once a day. The longer you leave it, the softer the mangoes will become. Once the jar is opened, keep it in the fridge. Should keep for at least a month – if you haven't finished it already!

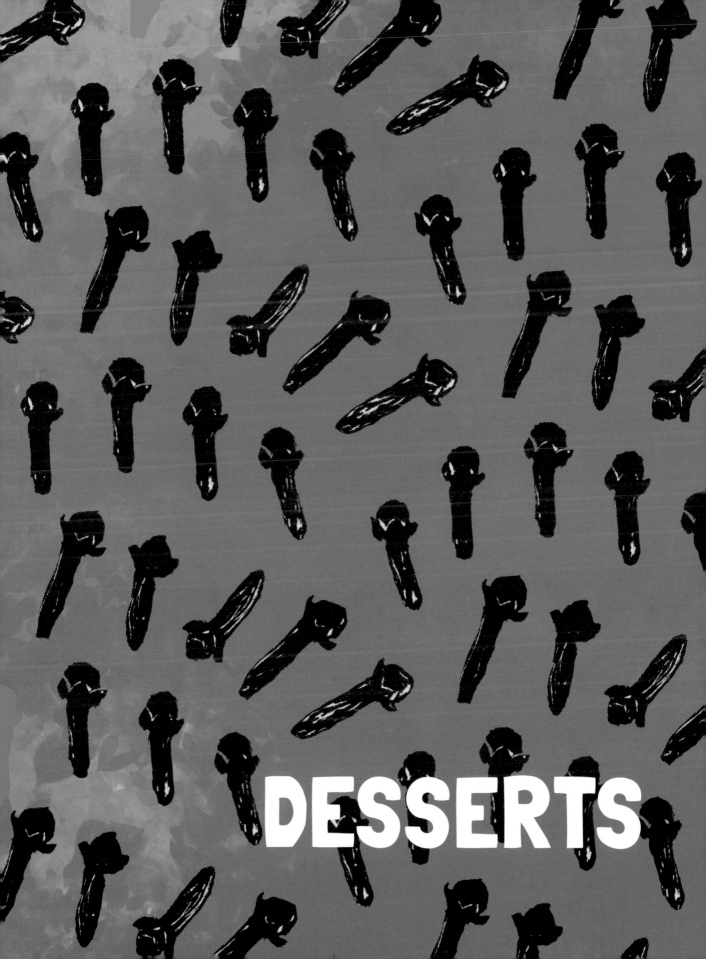

DESSERTS

Refreshing, fragrant and indulgent

This section includes the heavily sugar-laden mithai or, 'sweetmeats' as they are more commonly known here. You might be familiar with the milky barfi, often cut into diamond or square shapes, or the lurid orange jalebis, shaped into curly-wurly doodles. Also well known are the milk-based gulab jamun, round brown deep-fried balls, or rasgullas, kneaded paneer balls, both of which are poached in a fragrantly spicy syrup. Spices such as saffron, cardamom and cinnamon are often used in their preparation to add both flavour and aroma.

These delicacies are consumed in huge quantities on festive celebrations such as Diwali (festival of lights), Holi (festival of colours) and Lohri (winter solstice). They are served in Gurdwaras or presented in decorative boxes as gifts on special occasions such as weddings and birthday parties, or even passing an exam or a driving test. Likewise, they are offered to welcome family and friends into your home, to show that you honour and respect them as your guests. In fact, any excuse can be used to pop one in your mouth...

Some Indian desserts can almost be a meal on their own, as they are rich and nourishing with milk, butter, sugar and nuts. If you've had a lavish meal, you may be full by the end of it and prefer something refreshing like fruit chaat.

But there is a wide variety of desserts for you to choose from in this section, so enjoy – in moderation!

FRUIT CHAAT

Fruit salad with a sprinkling of spices

This spice mix seems an improbable combination with fruit but it really works. You'll be surprised at how much the tangy, salty chaat enhances the sweetness of the fruit. Almost any array of fruit will prove successful, but I particularly recommend the inclusion of fruit such as pineapple, mango, melon or papaya. I have experimented using English fruit: apples and pears in autumn are perfect, but strawberries and raspberries in summer don't seem quite right.

There aren't really any set quantities for this recipe so it just depends on your personal preference. In fact, you could just invite your fellow diners to take as much masala as they want. If you feel a bit more adventurous, try replacing the lime or lemon with a couple of tablespoons of tamarind chutney (page 214).

Serves 6

Select enough fruit for 6 people
   (about 1kg in total)
1 tsp or more *chaat masala*
   (page 254)
juice of 1 lemon or lime

Slice or chop the fruit, place in a shallow dish and sprinkle lightly with the masala. Pour the juice over and serve.

SHRIKHAND
Pomegranate and yogurt dessert

Crunchy pomegranate, fragrant saffron and smooth yogurt. For me, this dessert will always be associated with a freezing December bike ride to my friend Bina's house on my birthday. The wiser amongst us drove there and the more foolhardy cycled in just T-shirts and shorts. However, our perseverance paid off as we were rewarded with a fantastic lunch, capped by this simple but mouth-watering dessert.

Prepare a few hours – or even a day – ahead, to really let the flavours and deep orange colour of the saffron infuse into the yogurt.

Serves 6-8

1kg *Greek-style yogurt* (page 222)
3 tbsp icing sugar, sieved
1 pomegranate,
  skin and pith removed
2 tbsp flaked almonds
juice of 1 lemon

a pinch of saffron strands
1 tsp green cardamom pods, husks
  removed and seeds finely ground
2 tbsp unsalted pistachios,
  chopped or thinly sliced

Put the yogurt into a bowl and stir in the icing sugar until thoroughly mixed.

Add the pomegranate, almonds, lemon juice and saffron. Gently mix together. Scoop into a serving dish or individual dishes and garnish with the cardamom and pistachios.

GAJARELA
Carrot pudding

This Punjabi pudding is a treat for lovers of carrots – fragrantly spiced and indulgently garnished with almonds, pistachios and cardamom. Don't take any short cuts – gold top milk is the only one to choose if you want to stay true to this dish. Serve on its own, with cream, or, to be really decadent, with kulfi (page 240).

Serves 6

80g unsalted butter
5 cloves
800g carrots, coarsely grated
500ml full cream milk,
    preferably gold top
a pinch of saffron strands
50g caster sugar

1 tbsp green cardamom pods,
    husks removed and seeds
    finely ground
2 tbsp blanched almonds,
    chopped or thinly sliced
2 tbsp unsalted pistachios,
    chopped or thinly sliced

Melt the butter in a large saucepan on a gentle heat. Add the cloves. Turn the heat to medium and add the carrots, a handful at a time, stirring for about 20 seconds after each time to prevent them from becoming mushy. Stir constantly for about 10 minutes until they are coated in the butter and quite dry.

Add the milk and bring to the boil. Add the saffron, sugar and half of the ground cardamom. Half cover the pan with a lid and simmer for about 15 minutes, or longer for a thicker consistency. Serve garnished with the almonds, pistachios and the remainder of the cardamom.

KULFI
Indian ice cream

The first time I can remember having kulfi was on a trip to India in my teens. We were staying in New Delhi before journeying on to the Punjab, and the daughters of our family friends took me out for the evening. They sometimes visited us in England when I was young, and I always thought they were really trendy with their strong Delhi accents, which I love hearing to this day. They took me to the local 'cool' places and we finished the evening at an ice-cream parlour. Being young in such a vibrant city with all its colours, smells, sounds and mysticism, was hugely exciting, and this wonderful ice cream added the finishing touch to my adventure. Made in aluminium cone-shaped moulds and served on a wooden stick, the kulfi was rich, fragrant and smooth.

To make this, don't take shortcuts by using cream, as only full cream milk will give you the dense texture that is so reminiscent of kulfi. You need to stir the milk frequently otherwise it will burn, and don't rush the boiling process. To achieve the nutty caramelised flavour, it needs to be cooked on a slow, gentle heat and reduced to about half its original quantity – and that takes time.

Serves 8-10

2 litres full cream milk,
    preferably gold top
150g caster sugar
5 green cardamom pods,
    husks removed and seeds
    finely ground

1 tbsp blanched almonds, chopped
1 tbsp unsalted pistachios,
    chopped
a few pistachios, almonds and
    cardamom pods, prepared as
    above, to garnish

Bring the milk to the boil in a heavy-bottomed saucepan and simmer for about two to two and a half hours until it has reduced by half. After about an hour, add the sugar and cardamom. Stir often to prevent the milk from sticking to the bottom of the pan and to ensure that any skin that has formed on top is mixed in.

Remove from the heat. Whisk lightly with a fork. Stir in the almonds and pistachios, then leave to cool. Pour into a freezer-proof container or individual moulds, and place in the freezer until completely frozen.

Remove from the freezer 5 minutes before serving. Garnish with the remaining pistachios, almonds and cardamom.

RASGULLAS
Paneer balls in an aromatic syrup

This recipe almost didn't make it into the book. I'd invited my friends over for lunch and we planned to finish the meal with these paneer balls. I hadn't prepared them for years but was feeling rather pleased with myself as they looked perfect. As everyone spooned in, I realised that the rasgullas were what I can only describe as rock hard. Obviously, I had to give it another go to convince everyone that this recipe would work – if I could just figure out what went wrong. So again I turned to my massis (aunts) for help. The problem was I hadn't kneaded the paneer long enough for the grainy texture to disappear. I made a further attempt with a few tweaks and they all turned out just right. So here they are – my perfected rasgullas!

Serves 6-8

150-180g *crumbly paneer*
(page 257-8)

For the syrup
1 litre water
100g granulated sugar
1 tsp green cardamom pods, husks removed and seeds finely ground
10 cloves
1 cinnamon stick, about 5cm

Knead the paneer until all the grains disappear, then shape into 10-12 balls of about 3cm diameter. Set aside.

Put all the ingredients for the syrup into a large saucepan with a tight-fitting lid. Bring the water to the boil over a medium heat and then continue to simmer for 20-30 minutes until it has thickened and has the consistency of a thin syrup. Lower the heat and carefully place the balls into the pan. Cover and poach for 15-20 minutes. When done, they will float to the surface. If the syrup begins to thicken, add some splashes of water. Cool the rasgullas before placing in the fridge to chill.

Serve one or two rasgullas per person, spooning a little of the syrup – including the spices – over each one.

KHEER
Rice pudding

This rich and creamy pudding is typical of North Indian cuisine. We always made it at home to celebrate the birthday of Guru Nanak, the founder of the Sikh religion. Gurpurab, as it is called, usually falls in November on the full moon day in the month of Kartik in the Indian lunar calendar. With the nights drawing in and the air outside already cold, we would settle down to the cosy warmth of the kheer. In the Gurdwaras, it is made in huge vats and served to the congregation for weddings and special days in the religious calendar. It is usually served with nuts and dried fruit but I've also seen it with chopped fresh fruit (banana, mango and pineapple), though I find this option less appealing. Take your pick. Just remember that the pudding will thicken slightly as it cools, so be careful not to overcook it or you'll end up with a solid mass.

Serves 6

100g basmati rice,
   rinsed and soaked in
   cold water for 30 minutes
1 litre whole milk
60g caster sugar
3 tbsp blanched almonds,
   chopped or thinly sliced

2 tbsp unsalted pistachios,
   chopped or thinly sliced
1 tbsp green cardamom pods,
   husks removed and seeds
   finely ground
1 tbsp sultanas or raisins (optional)

Rinse and drain the rice thoroughly.

Put the rice into a large saucepan. Add the milk and caster sugar and bring to the boil. Turn down the heat and cover with a lid, leaving a small gap. Simmer for about 20-25 minutes, longer if you want it really thick. Stir occasionally to prevent it sticking to the bottom of the pan. Stir in the almonds, pistachios, cardamom and dried fruit. Serve.

BESAN
Indian-style fudge

Besan really brings childhood memories to mind. A treasure best summed up as rich, mellow, and melt-in-the-mouth sweet. My mum had two days off from work each week and very often they would fall on weekdays. On those days I would race home from school, not only for the pleasure of seeing her, but also because she might have prepared something special for me and my brothers to eat. Besan was one of those delights and I absolutely loved it. My recipe includes a mere 150g of flour, but I'm sure my mum's version used closer to a kilo. Looking back, I feel slightly embarrassed because I was the family member who ate almost all of it, though not in one go. My only excuse is that I used up vast amounts of energy running home!

You can vary the texture by using either granulated sugar to make it grainy, or powdery icing sugar to make it smoother. Adding a little more butter will make it softer. Whichever one you choose, there is no right or wrong way. To shape and set the besan, I use two 12cm diameter flan tins with removable bases, as it's then easier to cut into little pieces. Give it a go and be patient, because you really do need to stir it non-stop or it will burn. Keep in an airtight container and eat within a few days when it's at its freshest. Serve with tea or as an after-dinner treat with coffee.

Don't be confused by the name – the fudge has the same name as the flour used to make it.

Serves 8-10

100g unsalted butter
150g gram flour (besan), sieved
75g granulated sugar or
  icing sugar
1 tbsp green cardamom pods,
  husks removed and seeds
  finely ground

1 tbsp blanched almonds,
  chopped or thinly sliced
1 tbsp unsalted pistachios,
  chopped or thinly sliced
2 x 12cm loose-bottomed
  flan tins, lightly greased
  with butter

Melt the butter in a medium-sized karahi or frying pan on a low heat. Add the flour to the pan and stir constantly for 20 minutes. The dry, crumbly mixture will become smoother as the butter separates from it. The raw smell of the flour will change to a mellow nutty aroma as it roasts with the butter and it will turn from a pale yellow to a deep golden brown. The texture will be similar to wet sand. Keep an eye on it, as it will burn easily. Stir in the sugar and cardamom until completely absorbed into the mixture. It will now resemble a thick paste.

Press into your buttered tins. Sprinkle the almonds and pistachios over and then, using the back of a spoon, press down gently onto the besan. Leave to cool and set for an hour or two. Remove from the tins and cut into little triangles, diamonds or squares.

SEVIAN
Vermicelli pudding

This pudding makes a very special finale for a dinner party. Oddly enough, I also used to enjoy it for breakfast. On cold mornings, it warmed me up before my trek to school. I usually serve the almonds, pistachios and cardamom separately in little bowls so people can help themselves to as much or as little as they want.

The dish will thicken as it cools so be careful not to overcook it otherwise you'll end up with a solid mass.

Serves 6

20g butter
5 nests of vermicelli
5 cloves
1 cinnamon stick, about 5cm
1.2 litres whole milk
80g caster sugar

3 tbsp blanched almonds,
  chopped or thinly sliced
3 tbsp unsalted pistachios,
  chopped or thinly sliced
1 tbsp green cardamom pods,
  husks removed and seeds
  finely ground

Melt the butter in a large saucepan over a low heat. Break the nests of vermicelli into the pan, stirring all the time until the strands are completely coated with the butter.

Add the cloves, cinnamon, milk and caster sugar, continuing to stir gently. Bring to the boil and then simmer for 10 minutes or until the vermicelli is soft and the milk has thickened a little. Serve garnished with the almonds, pistachios and cardamom.

A family group photo, Hounslow, Middlesex (1971) – I'm on the far left

GLOSSARY OF INGREDIENTS

Herbs and spices make up the bulk of the ingredients listed below (with italics for the others) and I wanted to say a quick word about them first.

Particular spices are associated with regional cuisines. In the Punjab region of northern India, for example, garam masala is appreciated for its robust earthy tones and used abundantly. Further to the west, in Gujarat, the strong distinctive tastes of asafoetida, mustard seeds and curry (neem) leaves impart completely different flavours, often counterbalanced with hints of sweet and sour to create a unique style of cooking. In the southern region of Kerala, pepper, cloves, cinnamon and tamarind are widely grown and are often combined with coconut to flavour the fish and seafood for which this region is famed. Luckily for us, even though some of these spices are shared all over India, the multitude of combinations creates an endless variety of dishes.

Learning to differentiate between herbs and spices and how to use them will come with time and experience. Remember, their role is to enhance and complement the flavour of the food. Of course, they come in various forms: herbs (fresh or dried), seeds (whole or ground), bark (cinnamon), fruit (tamarind) or root (ginger). You'll find that crushing or grinding the spices will produce different flavours and aromas. How you prepare your ingredients will affect how your dish turns out.

Tempering (by frying in hot oil) brings out the colour, aroma and intensity of the spices. Another important element in their use is the order in which they are added during the cooking process. Spices are generally introduced at the beginning, to slowly develop the depth of flavour of the dish, whereas herbs are more often added towards the end, to impart freshness and colour.

I prefer to grind my own spices rather than use shop-bought, as the flavour and aroma is always fresher and more intense. It's up to you whether you do things the traditional way, with a pestle and mortar, or use a grinding machine. However, if using your coffee grinder, you'll need to clean it thoroughly if you don't want your 'cuppa' to taste of spices. Store your ingredients in glass jars, or a masala dhaba (spice box, page 267) and keep in a dark place, such as a cupboard, to help retain their flavour.

You'll probably find it useful to know how to create your own 'masalas' (blend of spices) so this section also includes the two used in this book, chaat masala and garam masala.

Almonds (badaam) - I often use these for flavouring desserts and garnishing. If you prefer, you can blanch your own at home by soaking them in hot water and then peeling off the skin. Alternatively, buy as flakes or ready-ground from the supermarket.

Asafoetida (hing) - its name, reminiscent of the word 'fetid', hints at its distinctive smell, so it's best to store it separately in a tight-fitting jar, rather than in your spice box, as it will overpower all your other spices. It comes from the gum extracted from a perennial plant and is dried and ground to a powder. I wouldn't use this spice without frying it first in hot oil. Tempering it helps transform it to a smooth sweet tasting spice that I use in my Gujarati recipes.

Bay leaf (tejpatta) - a surprisingly pervasive and subtle herb, used whole to flavour meat and rice. You may wish to experiment with the Indian bay leaf, which has a different flavour, although I am perfectly content to use the European variety.

Black cardamom (kali elachi) - used in meat dishes, desserts and tea. Used whole, it is for flavouring a dish and not for eating. It is quite different from green cardamom (see below) and has a flavour rather like wood smoke, perhaps with a hint of aniseed. A key ingredient in garam masala (see below).

Black mustard seeds (rai) - exist in three colours: yellow, brown and black, the last of these being the strongest in flavour. They are fiery and pungent until tempered in oil, which releases their fragrant smokiness. If you only have yellow seeds, just use a few more to strengthen the flavour of your dish.

Black pepper (kali mirch) - used whole, it gives a fiery burst of sensation on the palate. Gives garam masala (see below) its kick.

Black salt (kala loon) - has a sharp and refreshing tangy flavour. It's used to season savoury dishes and is also a vital ingredient in chaat masala (see below). It isn't actually black - more a pinkish grey colour!

Carom seeds (ajwain) - similar in appearance to cumin seeds but smaller and more bitter. Often used to flavour Indian pickles. Also used in the preparation of tea (ajwain chai).

Chaat masala - a sherbet-tangy blend of spices, often used as a topping for salads – whether vegetable or fruit – and particularly in "street food" preparations. The tartness of the black salt and mango powder, combined with the piquancy of the chilli, is counter-balanced with the earthiness of the coriander and cumin. Sprinkle sparingly on your favourite fruit with a drizzle of tamarind chutney or lemon juice.

1 tbsp ground coriander
1 tbsp ground cumin
1 tsp mango powder
1 tsp black salt powder
a pinch of chilli flakes

Warm a small pan over a low heat and then dry roast the coriander and cumin for 30 seconds or until they deepen in colour and give off a mellow fragrance. Remove from the heat and place in a bowl to cool completely. Add the remainder of the ingredients. Mix thoroughly. Store in a glass jar.

Chapati flour (atta) - made from Indian durum wheat and used to prepare unleavened flatbread commonly referred to as roti, chapati or phulka. Chapati flour can be purchased in Asian stores where it will already have the correct mix of wholemeal and white flour. See the recipes in the section on Rice and breads for its preparation.

Chilli (mirch) - used fresh in all shapes and sizes and with varying degrees of 'heat'. I put out a small bowl of fresh chillies with just about every meal I serve. For those of us from an Indian background, to perspire a little from eating good chillies is often seen as a highly desirable part of the dining experience! Dried chillies are often fried in hot oil to bring out their flavour. Chilli flakes or powder, meanwhile, can be used in many different ways: for example, in marinades, sauces and pickles, or even as a garnish for fruit salad, as above (in the chaat masala recipe).

We always have chilli plants growing in our garden in the summer and pots are promptly brought in when the season is over, so we can continue to enjoy them for a little longer in the colder months. Any excess chillies are dried, stored and then ground coarsely to produce something that's halfway between flakes and powder.

Cinnamon (dalchini) - deceptively sweet, despite its appearance, and used in both sweet and savoury recipes. A key element in garam masala, where it complements some of the spicier ingredients.

Cloves (laung) - a warm and fragrant aroma with a somewhat peppery taste. They can be used in both savoury and sweet recipes.

Coconut (nariyal) - sometimes used fresh as a garnish for desserts. In this book, it is used either desiccated or as coconut milk. Used widely in Keralan cuisine.

Coriander (dhaniya) - lightly crushing the seeds enhances its floral spiciness. When ground, its flavour is toned down to give a slightly earthy bitterness. Its fresh leaves make an attractive garnish to many dishes and provide a refreshing, lemony contrast to the stronger spices. Although they look similar, don't mistake (or be tempted to swap) parsley for coriander, as they taste completely different.

Cumin (jeera) - looks a bit like carom but the seeds are bigger and it's less bitter. Used in most Indian dishes, and often tempered in oil at the start of a recipe, it releases an enticing savoury fragrance.

Curry leaf (neem) - a small green elongated thin leaf used in my Gujarati recipes. The leaves are usually fried lightly in hot oil to release a slightly sweet aroma. Often tempered with asafoetida and mustard seeds. You can sometimes buy the fresh leaves in Indian supermarkets but more often you will only find the dried form, which works equally well.

Fennel (saunf) - very aromatic with a sweet flavour a little like anise. It's used in tea, desserts and as a breath freshener.

Fenugreek (methi) - grew abundantly in our garden as I was growing up. My mum sometimes dried the leaves so that we had a full supply for winter, and I remember trays of fenugreek lying in the sunshine. The seeds are usually tempered in oil to release their flavour. Fenugreek has a strong, rather bitter, taste so don't go overboard with it. Once you are familiar with the taste, and like it, you could try including it in more of the recipes.

Garam masala - a combination of spices used in most Punjabi dishes – although every Punjabi household most likely has its own unique blend. This is the one I grew up with, watching my mum grind the spices for hours with a huge pestle and mortar. Nowadays, I let the coffee grinder do the work. Mind you, I ended up buying an extra grinder to keep the taste of spices out of my coffee!

The quality of the garam masala will depend on the freshness of the spices. A little more or less of any one of the ingredients won't affect the end result too much but don't stray too far from this recipe. It will keep for up to 2 months or so in a sealed jar but it will start to lose its colour and aroma over time. You can buy garam masala at supermarkets but it'll never taste as good as the homemade version. It's also very simple to make… but be warned – it might make you sneeze while you're preparing it!

1 cinnamon stick, 6-8cm
5 black cardamom pods
2 tbsp cumin seeds
2 tbsp coriander seeds
1 tbsp black peppercorns
1 tbsp cloves

Grind all the spices together until they are quite fine.

Garlic (lasan) - as indispensable as ginger and chilli in Indian cooking. More often than not, all three are added to the pan at the same time, which is why you will see them so often grouped together in the recipes. Care should be taken when using it as the high sugar content means it burns easily.

Ghee - a type of clarified butter that has been melted and the milk solids removed, leaving it looking slightly oily but with a richly aromatic and nutty flavour. Delicious with whole urid dhal (page 110).

Ginger (adrak) - has a wonderfully sharp, tangy flavour. Unless the ginger is very fresh and clean, I recommend peeling it.

Gram flour (besan) - chickpea flour, but not from the white chickpeas used to make hummus. Gram flour is produced from black chickpeas that have been dehusked and ground. The flour is usually either mixed with water to make a batter or combined with chapati flour to make unleavened flatbread.

Green cardamom (elachi) - has sweet, aromatic, strong seeds that can be used in both savoury and sweet dishes. They are very popular (with the outer husk still on) in India as mouth fresheners. Press down with a rolling pin or lightly squash with a pestle and mortar to remove the husk.

Mango powder (amchoor) - a spice with a sharp and fruity flavour. Made from dried green mangoes (page 258), it adds a citrusy dimension to 'earthy' tasting dishes. It is a key ingredient for making chaat masala.

Mint (podina) - a fresh tasting herb used in raita and biryanis. It also makes a fine chutney and is a welcome garnish for savoury dishes or a fruit salad.

Nigella seeds (kalonji) - a bitter and woody tasting spice often seen on naans. Widely used in the preparation of chutneys and pickles.

Oil (tel) - I use extra virgin olive oil for general stovetop cooking. For deep-frying I use sunflower oil, but an oil of your choice (suitable for a high temperature) will work too. See also Cooking tips (pages 263-4).

Paneer - creamy, unfermented Indian cheese, a bit like feta cheese in terms of texture. Like lentils and beans, it's a source of protein for vegetarians. As it doesn't need to mature, you can make it and use it immediately. It's very versatile in Indian cuisine, used in savoury and sweet dishes alike, and can be cubed, crumbled, fried, barbecued or sautéed. The weight of the finished paneer depends on how much liquid is drained out during its preparation, so there will be small variations in quantity.

It can generally be found at most supermarkets, but this recipe is simple and the results are very satisfying!

1 litre whole milk (makes about 150g)
juice of 1 or 2 lemons

Bring the milk to the boil in a large pan and turn off the heat. Squeeze the lemon juice into the milk and stir gently for a minute or so until the milk curdles (separates). If it doesn't separate, add a little more lemon juice. You'll know it's ready when the liquid changes to a yellowish green colour.

Line a metal sieve or colander with muslin (cheesecloth, a thin cotton tea towel or fine mesh cloth) and place over a large bowl. Strain the milk so the milk curds (solids) are left in the sieve and the whey (liquid) drains through into the bowl. If you like, you can rinse some of the lemon flavour away by running the mixture under cold water at this point. Leave it to cool for about 20 minutes. Draw the ends of the cloth together and squeeze out as much whey as possible – take care, as the paneer may still be hot. Leave to drain for an hour. Then follow one of the methods below depending on your recipe.

Paneer cubes
Flatten out into a rectangular shape about 2.5cm-thick. Wrap in the cloth and place on a plate. Put a heavy weight on the block of paneer (e.g. a pan) and leave in the fridge for 2-3 hours to drain any excess liquid from the curds. Cut into 2cm cubes. They will keep in the fridge for a few days.

Crumbly paneer
Gently rub the paneer, as you would with butter and flour to bake a cake, until it resembles breadcrumbs. This will keep in the fridge for a few days.

Paprika - mild, sweet, piquant, with a slightly woody taste. Its flavour varies a little depending on which variety you buy. It's often used to add colour to meat dishes.

Pistachio nuts (pista) - and almonds are traditionally often used together to flavour, garnish and enrich desserts.

Pomegranate (anardana) - gorgeous colour and sweet tartness for salads and desserts. When used as dried seeds or as a powder in chutneys, it loses some sweetness but gains in depth of fruity, spicy tanginess.

Pulses - tinned or dried. For vegetarians like me, lentils and beans are an important source of protein and I see them as the essence of Indian home cooking. See also the introduction to Pulses (page 101) for the different ways of preparing them.

Raw green mango (hari amb) - best known for its use in mango pickle, where its tart tangy flavour easily overrides all the other spices. Don't confuse it with the mango fruit varieties that come in shades of yellow, orange and red. This one is much smaller, the skin is light green and the flesh varies from white to a very pale yellow. It is often used in its dried form: mango powder (see above).

Rice (chaul) - long-grained, with a beautifully fragrant aroma, basmati is the only variety of rice that will give you the authentic flavour and texture you should enjoy with these recipes. It is easy to cook as long as you have the right ratio of rice to water. See also chaul recipe (page 196), introduction to Rice and breads (page 181) and Cooking tips (pages 263-4).

Saffron (kesar) - used in meat dishes and desserts. Collected from the saffron-crocus flower, which is a very labour-intensive plant to cultivate, it's often soaked in hot water or hot milk to intensify its colour and flowery flavour. Use it sparingly, as it's quite strong – and very expensive!

Salt (loon) - essential to bring out the flavour of the food. See also Cooking tips (pages 263-4).

Star anise - true to its name, this star-shaped spice adds a warm, sweet aniseed and liquorice flavour to dishes.

Sesame (til) - these seeds have a naturally nutty flavour that will be more pronounced after tempering. They are available in a variety of colours, any of which may be suitable, but I usually use the white ones that are most widely available. Be careful not to burn them because that will spoil the taste of your dish.

Tamarind (imli) - a fruit from the tamarind tree that is available in a number of different forms. Tamarind concentrate is much more convenient than the blocks of tamarind pulp, but don't be tempted to use the 'extract' because it's nowhere near as good. I love to use tamarind in chutneys and sauces or drizzled over fruit and salads to create a sweet and savoury flavour. It is used extensively in the preparation of Indian snacks. See the tamarind chutney recipe on page 214 to learn more about it.

Turmeric (haldi) - a spice with a bright orangey-yellow colour, usually found in powdered form. You need to be careful not to get it on your clothes because the stains are very hard to remove. The taste is sometimes described as a combination of orange and ginger, with a very slight bitterness. It lends an earthy aroma and distinctive colour to many Indian recipes.

Yogurt (dahi) - an important part of a traditional Punjabi meal, providing a natural balance to the spices. It can also be used in the cooking process to thin down sauces or to counteract over-spicing – just stir a little into the dish towards the end of the cooking time. See the yogurt recipe (page 222).

COOKING TIPS

Be brave - adjust the ingredients and quantities to cook for more or fewer people once you've mastered the dishes.

Cardamom - to split the pods, lightly bash with a rolling pin.

Chilli - I have specified amounts but add to taste.

Chop - I use a mini processor for ginger, garlic and chillies and a larger processor for onions.

Coriander leaves - if you're looking to add colour and freshness, then chopped coriander can be used to garnish most savoury dishes. Don't chop the leaves too finely, as they'll lose their fresh lemony flavour. If the stems are tender, I use those too.

Deep-fry - it's difficult to specify exactly how much oil to use as it will depend on the size of your pan but make sure you use enough to (at least half) cover what you're cooking. See also Oil below (page 264).

Flavour - to achieve the true flavour of the dishes you are preparing, follow the recipes closely and don't take short cuts.

Garam masala - add either during the cooking process or right at the end. Experiment to see which you prefer.

Garlic - I use fat cloves of garlic.

Ginger, **garlic**, **chilli** and **onion** - if they are beginning to stick to the pan, add a few splashes of water. See also Chop, above.

Grind - try to grind your own spices for freshness.

Heat diffuser - use for slow, gentle cooking. See also Cooking equipment (page 267).

Masala basic sauce - these recipes start with onion, ginger, garlic and chilli, followed by tomato. The consistency of the sauce will affect the final outcome of your dish, so don't stray from the instructions.

Measure - in a long recipe, measure the ingredients beforehand and have them ready in the order they are used.

Measurements - in each recipe, these are given in level spoons unless specified. See also Onion weights and Weights, below (pages 264-5).

Oil - if a recipe starts by heating oil, make sure it is hot before adding the spices so as to really bring out their flavour. All the recipes use vegetable oil. I tend to use extra virgin olive oil for general cooking. For deep-frying I use sunflower oil, but you can use any oil of your choice, providing that it withstands a high temperature. Always heat it gradually to prevent it from burning.

Onion weights - small 100g, medium 150g and large 200g.

Peas - I take peas out from the freezer when I start preparing a recipe, so they're almost defrosted by the time I need them.

Potatoes - usually, all-purpose potatoes are ideal for most of the recipes. I boil them in their skins because it makes them easier to peel, helps retain flavour and prevents them from going mushy.

Prawns - devein and butterfly. To do this, take a sharp knife, cut down through the back to the black 'vein' and prise it out. Now cut deeper along the back, without going all the way through, and open up the prawn.

Pulses - some of the beans, lentils and peas need to be soaked in water, so check the recipe well in advance.

Read - it's a good idea to read the recipe beforehand, particularly if preparations need to begin a few hours before or the day before.

Rice - basmati is the only one I use to prepare Indian food. Soak for 30 minutes and then drain thoroughly as this will help to separate the grains. A pan with a glass lid will help you see what the rice is doing. Leave the lid on while it is cooking and let it stand for at least 5 minutes before fluffing it up with a fork. See also introduction to Rice and breads (page 181).

Salt - has recently become a controversial ingredient in many ways. Personally, I would never cook without it, as I feel it brings out the flavour of the food.

Spices - all the spices are there for a reason and affect the final flavour of your dish, so do try to include them all.

Tempering - frying spices in hot oil brings out their flavour and aroma. With only seconds of difference in their cooking times, have the spices measured out and lined up in the order specified in the recipe. Heat the oil until it is just smoking and then add the spices in quick succession. Don't take your eyes off the pan as they will change from deliciously roasted to burnt and bitter.

Tomatoes: fresh, tinned or passata - if using fresh tomatoes, ripe ones are best. If I use tinned tomatoes, I whizz them first in the food processor or break them down with a wooden spoon when added to the pan. The type and quality of the tomatoes will affect the taste of the dish, so choose carefully. When adding tomatoes for a sauce, don't skimp on the cooking time because, in most cases, they need to be well-cooked to achieve the deep and true flavour of your dish.

Weights - weights of ingredients in these recipes are given prior to their preparation. See also Measurements and Onion weights, above.

Whole spices - used to add flavour to a dish. If you come across any while eating, just put them on the side of your plate.

Yogurt - add to thin a sauce or stir in a little if your dish is too salty.

COOKING EQUIPMENT

Along with the everyday utensils you would find in a kitchen, some of the following might come in handy.

Electric grinder - a 'must' if you want to grind your own spices, which will be fresher and tastier than the shop-bought options.

Food processor or **mini chopper** - useful to blend tomatoes and to chop onions, ginger, garlic and chillies.

Heat diffuser - this has become indispensable in my kitchen. It spreads the heat so that your food is cooked evenly. Very handy when preparing recipes that require a long cooking time or a low heat.

Karahi - a heavy-bottomed pan with steep sides, similar in shape to a wok, that suits the Indian style of shallow cooking and deep-frying. It can be purchased in most large Asian supermarkets.

Masala dhaba - a round steel tin containing small cups to store your most frequently used spices.

Muslin - cheesecloth, thin cotton tea towel or fine-mesh cloth – to make paneer.

Pans - good quality, heavy-bottomed pans can be used in place of a karahi.

Pestle and mortar - to grind spices and nuts and to prepare chutneys the traditional way.

Rolling pin - or belna to roll the flatbreads.

Slotted spoon - to turn and lift, and to drain the excess oil from your deep-fried food.

Sieve - use a large sieve to wash rice, beans, lentils and peas or to drain off the whey (liquid) in paneer-making.

Splatter lid - particularly useful at the start of a recipe when tempering spices that spit and pop.

Tawa - a flat pan traditionally made of cast iron or steel to prepare flatbreads. A heavy-bottomed frying pan made of similar material will work just as well. See also the chapati recipe (page 182).

INDEX

THANKS

To all my dear family and friends who have encouraged and supported me over the past few years:

Biji – my wonderful mother.

Dan, for being the first person to follow Biji's chicken recipe. Aunty Jeeta, Rani, Lesley and Nadia, for being my expert besan tasters. Amana, for the feedback on the coconut and coriander chutney. Rosemary, for trying the rajmah. Pete and Tim, for the Sunday afternoon dhal. Anne and Mark, always keen to try new recipes. Monica, for cooking dinner for me. Hilary, for looking after me so warmly in Northumberland. Rob, for preparing all those lunches. Drew and Katy, for making the barbecue chicken, a favourite of yours. Atul, for following the recipes to a 'T'. Ofer, for the pilau. Linda, for being invited to dinner and then having to cook it all. Christine, for the New Year's Eve chilli paneer. Joe, for the five husks of vermicelli. Gurkiran, for being so willing to try out the recipes. Farhan and Ben, for testing the recipes in your cooking club. Balwinder, my cousin in India, for the mango pickle tips. My son Amar, always keen to 'try out' my recipes on his friends. Amar G, for the aloo papri chaat photo. Alex and Jo, for making the pomegranate dessert a part of your family's Sunday lunch. Sarah, Jayne, Hazel, Lisa, Kat, David and Ole, for all the adjectives – keep a look out for them. Lizzie, for your tips on putting the book together. Shreya and Niraj, for sharing your knowledge and recipes of Gujarati cooking. Ruben, for our chats about Keralan cuisine and the fisherman photo. Nick, Ruth and Phil, for the photography tips. Cathy, for the props, and Mark for my flattering portrait! My father, Dhiro massi, Surinder massi, and my cousin, Harpreet, for helping me with the Punjabi names for the recipes. Bina, for my birthday feast. Rohit, who hasn't stopped making garam masala! And to Boo and Ivor, for Nick, with lots of love.

My special thanks to all those who have helped me to create this book:

Gillian and Alison, for those fun cooking afternoons in the kitchen and for your enthusiasm and patience with me. Yael, for all your support throughout the project. Janki, for the beautiful artwork. Lindsey, Chris, Hilary and Abisola, for endless hours of proofreading. And to Colin, who has read 'allowing them to sizzle for a few seconds' almost as many times as I have – possibly more than he's had hot dinners!

Aran, for keeping me on track, for the beautiful photographs, and rescuing me from all my IT hiccups.

And lastly, to Aman's friends who have been so patient – it took time, but here it is!

Intro to writing   1st November 0?

He brought a pinch of spice to each
match. He injected fire into each of
the 80 minutes. His trademark more cast
memories of awe in my mind. The
side step genius - Jason Robinson.
I clearly remember thinking during
the semis of RWC 2007 how my
tv had broken. There was a quick
judder on the screen, I thought it had
misaligned or something! Really it
was JR whipping his feet, ball
and body from left to right so quickly
it took careful repeated playback to
believe.

Balwinder Kapila grew up in Hounslow, Middlesex. When she was only nine years old, she decided one day to prepare a surprise dinner of aloo gobi for when her mum returned from her shift at Heathrow. From then on, Balwinder went on to learn and master the secrets of her mother's cooking.

As she gained in knowledge, she became more confident in sharing her authentic Punjabi recipes and ingredients, as well as her inventive fusion dishes, incorporating influences from other parts of India and elsewhere.

Balwinder lives in Berkshire, not far from Reading; when she's not cooking and entertaining for family and friends, she loves to swim, cycle and take care of her garden.

This is her first book: a celebration of food, family and friendship.